Contents

Introduction to the course

Syllabus overview

This unit gives students a basic introduction to costing, introducing knowledge and skills which will be needed for Level 3 Management Accounting: Costing and Level 4 Management Accounting: Budgeting. Students will understand the importance of the costing system as a source of information for internal management decision-making. In contrast to the more outward perspective of financial accounting, the skills developed in this unit will allow students to provide information to managers that can be used to assist in internal business planning, decision making and control.

Test specification for this unit assessment

Assessment method	Marking type	Duration of assessment
Computer based assessment	Computer marked	1.5 hours

Learning outcomes	Weighting
1 Understand the cost recording system within an organisation	20%
2 Use cost recording techniques	60%
3 Provide information on actual and budgeted costs and income	20%
Total	**100%**

Assessment structure

1 ½ hours duration

Competency is 70%

Note. That this is only a guideline as to what might come up. The format and content of each task may vary from what we have listed below.

Your assessment will consist of 15 tasks

Task	Expected content	Max marks	Chapter ref	Study complete
Task 1	**Costing themes and financial accounting v cost accounting** True or false statements about costing themes such as variances, direct costs, cost behaviour and labour costs. Characteristics of financial and management accounting.	8	Cost classification Cost behaviour Labour costs and overheads Variances	
Task 2	**Cost behaviour, cost elements and direct v indirect costs** Selecting correct cost behaviour for different costs. Classifying costs by their element. Selecting whether particular costs are direct or indirect costs.	8	Cost classification Cost behaviour	
Task 3	**Coding** Selecting correct codes for transactions.	6	Coding costs	
Task 4	**Cost behaviour** Selecting the correct cost behaviour based on cost and level of activity. Use of high low method to calculate costs for particular activity levels.	12	Cost behaviour	
Task 5	**Overhead absorption rates and unit cost calculations** Overhead absorption rate calculations based on machine hours, labour hours and number of units. Unit cost calculation using direct costs and overheads.	12	Labour costs and overheads	

Task	Expected content	Max marks	Chapter ref	Study complete
Task 6	**Total cost and unit cost** Calculation of total costs and unit costs using fixed cost and variable cost information.	12	Cost behaviour	
Task 7	**Manufacturing account** Reordering costs into manufacturing account. Calculating cost totals for the manufacturing account.	14	Inventory classification and valuation	
Task 8	**Inventory valuation** Calculations of closing inventory and issue valuation using FIFO, LIFO and AVCO.	9	Inventory classification and valuation	
Task 9	**Inventory valuation** Calculations of closing inventory and issue valuation using FIFO, LIFO and AVCO.	12	Inventory classification and valuation	
Task 10	**Labour costs** Hourly pay and bonus calculations. Basic wage, overtime and gross wage calculations.	8	Labour costs and overheads	
Task 11	**Labour costs** Hourly pay and bonus calculations. Piecework wage calculations.	8	Labour costs and overheads	
Task 12	**Variance analysis** True/false statements about variances. Variance calculations and determining whether they are favourable or adverse.	9	Variances	
Task 13	**Variance analysis** Variance calculations and determining whether they are favourable or adverse.	8	Variances	

AAT

Elements of Costing

Level 2

Foundation Certificate in

Accounting

Course Book

Third edition 2018

ISBN 9781 5097 1822 1
ISBN (for internal use only) 9781 5097 1818 4

British Library Cataloguing-in-Publication Data
A catalogue record for this book is available from the British Library

Published by

BPP Learning Media Ltd
BPP House, Aldine Place
142-144 Uxbridge Road
London W12 8AA

www.bpp.com/learningmedia

Printed in the United Kingdom

BPP
LEARNING MEDIA

Task	Expected content	Max marks	Chapter ref	Study complete
Task 14	**Variance analysis** Variance calculations and calculations of variances as a percentage of budget.	6	Variances	
Task 15	**Variance analysis** Calculations of variances as a percentage of budget and deciding whether they are significant or not significant. Who to report variances to.	8	Variances	

Skills bank

Our experience of preparing students for this type of assessment suggests that to obtain competency, you will need to develop a number of key skills.

What do I need to know to do well in the assessment?

This unit is one of the mandatory Level 2 units. It introduces costing principles and prepares you to be a valuable member of a management accounting finance team.

To be successful in the assessment you need to:

- Understand the fundamental decisions and basic thinking behind different costing principles.

- Apply the techniques to 'real life' situations. These will generally be tested in numerical questions.

Assessment style

In the assessment you will complete tasks by:

1   Entering narrative by selecting from drop down menus of narrative options known as **picklists**

2   Using **drag and drop** menus to enter narrative

3   Typing in numbers or cost codes, known as **gapfill** entry

4   Entering **ticks**

5   Entering **dates** by selecting from a calendar

You must familiarise yourself with the style of the online questions and the AAT software before taking the assessment. As part of your revision, login to the **AAT website** and attempt their **online practice assessments**.

Introduction to the assessment

The question practice you do will prepare you for the format of tasks you will see in the *Elements of Costing* assessment. It is also useful to familiarise yourself with the introductory information you **may** be given at the start of the assessment. For example:

Each task is independent. You will not need to refer to your answers to previous tasks.

Read every task carefully to make sure you understand what is required.

Where the date is relevant, it is given in the task data.

Both minus signs and brackets can be used to indicate negative numbers UNLESS task instructions say otherwise.

You must use a full stop to indicate a decimal point. For example, write 100.57 NOT 100,57 OR 100 57.

You may use a comma to indicate a number in the thousands, but you don't have to. For example, 10000 and 10,000 are both acceptable.

Other indicators are not compatible with the computer-marked system.

Complete all 15 tasks

The tasks are set in a business situation where the following apply:

- You are employed by the business, Gold, as a bookkeeper.

- Gold uses a manual accounting system.

- Double entry takes place in the general ledger. Individual accounts of trade receivables and trade payables are kept in the sales and purchases ledgers as memorandum accounts.

- The cash book and petty cash book should be treated as part of the double entry system unless the task instructions say otherwise.

- The VAT rate is 20%.

1   As you revise, use the **BPP Passcards** to consolidate your knowledge. They are a pocket-sized revision tool, perfect for packing in that last-minute revision.

2   Attempt as many tasks as possible in the **Question Bank**. There are plenty of assessment-style tasks which are excellent preparation for the real assessment.

3   Always **check** through your own answers as you will in the real assessment, before looking at the solutions in the back of the Question Bank.

Key to icons

Key term

A key definition which is important to be aware of for the assessment

Formula to learn

A formula you will need to learn as it will not be provided in the assessment

Formula provided

A formula which is provided within the assessment and generally available as a pop-up on screen

Activity

An example which allows you to apply your knowledge to the technique covered in the Course Book. The solution is provided at the end of the chapter

Illustration

A worked example which can be used to review and see how an assessment question could be answered

Assessment focus point

A high priority point for the assessment

Open book reference

Where use of an open book will be allowed for the assessment

Real life examples

A practical real life scenario

AAT qualifications

The material in this book may support the following AAT qualifications:

AAT Foundation Certificate in Accounting Level 2, AAT Foundation Certificate in Accounting at SCQF Level 5 and AAT Foundation Diploma in Accounting and Business Level 2.

Supplements

From time to time we may need to publish supplementary materials to one of our titles. This can be for a variety of reasons, from a small change in the AAT unit guidance to new legislation coming into effect between editions.

You should check our supplements page regularly for anything that may affect your learning materials. All supplements are available free of charge on our supplements page on our website at:

www.bpp.com/learning-media/about/students

Improving material and removing errors

There is a constant need to update and enhance our study materials in line with both regulatory changes and new insights into the assessments.

From our team of authors BPP appoints a subject expert to update and improve these materials for each new edition.

Their updated draft is subsequently technically checked by another author and from time to time non-technically checked by a proof reader.

We are very keen to remove as many numerical errors and narrative typos as we can but given the volume of detailed information being changed in a short space of time we know that a few errors will sometimes get through our net.

We apologise in advance for any inconvenience that an error might cause. We continue to look for new ways to improve these study materials and would welcome your suggestions. Please feel free to contact our AAT Head of Programme at nisarahmed@bpp.com if you have any suggestions for us.

Introduction to costing systems

Learning outcomes

1.3	Identify the relationship between the costing and financial accounting systems within an organisation
	• Costing and financial accounting systems within an organisation
1.4	Identify sources of information about income and expenditure
	• How historic cost is used for accounting and cost reporting
	• How costing systems use actual or budgeted costs to determine unit/job cost
	• How budgeted and actual costs are used for planning and control purposes

Assessment context

Assessment questions will test your understanding of costing systems.

Qualification context

Understanding management accounting and costing is fundamental for qualifying as an Accounting Technician.

Business context

This section introduces you to the different type of costing systems used by business. You may already be familiar with some of these concepts.

Chapter overview

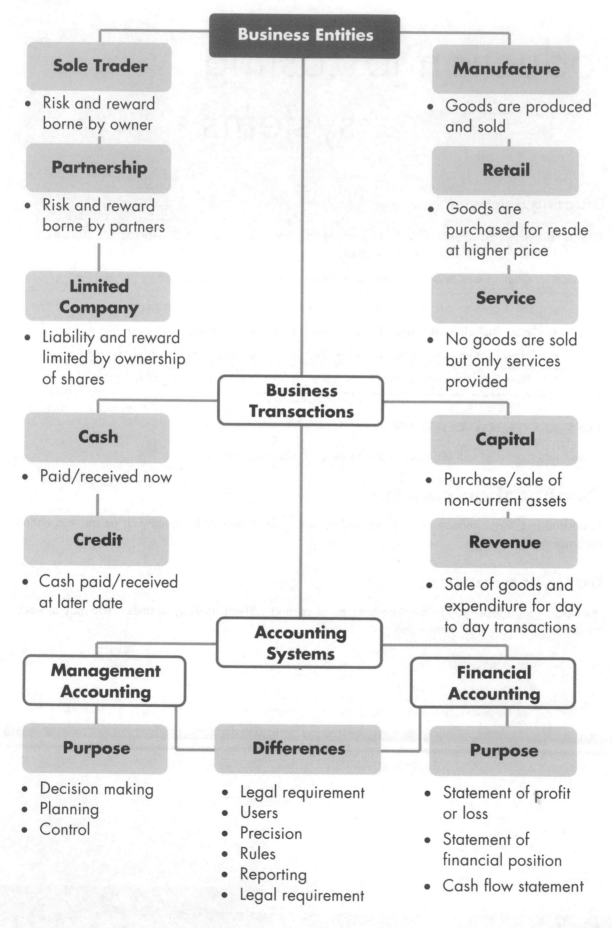

Business Entities

Sole Trader
- Risk and reward borne by owner

Partnership
- Risk and reward borne by partners

Limited Company
- Liability and reward limited by ownership of shares

Manufacture
- Goods are produced and sold

Retail
- Goods are purchased for resale at higher price

Service
- No goods are sold but only services provided

Business Transactions

Cash
- Paid/received now

Credit
- Cash paid/received at later date

Capital
- Purchase/sale of non-current assets

Revenue
- Sale of goods and expenditure for day to day transactions

Accounting Systems

Management Accounting

Financial Accounting

Purpose
- Decision making
- Planning
- Control

Differences
- Legal requirement
- Users
- Precision
- Rules
- Reporting
- Legal requirement

Purpose
- Statement of profit or loss
- Statement of financial position
- Cash flow statement

Introduction

This opening chapter introduces you to different types of business entities. You will read about costing systems and how these record the activities of the business. The chapter is written for someone who is new to business, so if you are already familiar with these topics, use this chapter to refresh your memory.

1 Types of business entity

Business entities can be structured in various forms. The **sole trader** is the simplest of these forms.

(a) Sole trader

- An individual sets up the business on their own and contributes **capital** to the business.

- All risks and rewards are borne by the sole trader.

(b) Partnership

- A group of individuals (usually between 2 and 20 people) enter into a business together.

- Risks and rewards are shared between the partners.

(c) Limited company

- A separate legal entity from the owners is created.
- The company bears the risks and rewards.
- The owners of the business own the company's shares.
- The company is managed by directors.
- The directors and the owners are often different people.
- The owners have limited liability.

1.1 Limited liability

The main difference between the trading of a sole trader and a **partnership** on the one hand and a **limited company** on the other is the concept of limited liability. If the business of a sole trader or a partnership runs out of money and is declared bankrupt then the sole trader or partners are personally liable for any outstanding debts of the business. However, the shareholders of a company have limited liability, which means that once they have fully paid for their shares they cannot be called upon for any more money if the company runs out and is declared insolvent. All that they will lose is the amount that they have paid for their shares.

Activity 1: Types of business 1

A business entity is owned and run by Alfred, Betty and Gemma.

Required

What type of a business is this an example of?

- ☐ Sole trader
- ☐ Partnership
- ☐ Limited company

Activity 2: Types of business 2

Alfred, Betty and Gemma are shareholders in ABC Ltd.

Required

What type of a business is this an example of?

- ☐ Sole trader
- ☐ Partnership
- ☐ Limited company

2 Types of industry

Businesses can be classified by type. There are three main categories:

Manufacturer – where goods are made and then sold

Retailer – where goods are bought in and sold to the public at a higher price

Service – where there are no goods at all but some service is provided

3 Business transactions

Whether a business is run as a sole trader, partnership or company, it will still carry out all the same types of business transaction, although on different scales.

Typical transactions that businesses undertake include the following:

- Buying materials to make goods
- Making goods
- Selling goods or services
- Buying goods to resell

- Paying expenses

- Paying wages

- Buying items like furniture, vans or a building (known as non-current assets) for use in the business in the long term

- Paying money into the bank

- Withdrawing cash from the bank

- Paying the owners (as either drawings or dividends)

- Paying taxes such as sales tax (VAT)

Each transaction must be correctly recorded in the accounting records of the business, and much of this is what will be covered in your studies.

As well as recording the everyday transactions, the accounting records provide valuable information to the owners or managers of the business. The records should indicate:

- How much money is owed by the business and to whom
- How much money is owed to the business and from whom
- What non-current assets the business has
- How much inventory the business holds

If the business is to run efficiently the accounting records must be capable of providing accurate information on all these areas.

3.1 Cash and credit transactions

Cash transactions are where payment is made or received **immediately**. The method of payment can include notes and coins, cheques, credit card and debit card.

Credit transactions are where goods or services are given or received now but payment for them is to be made or received at an agreed future date.

When a sale is made, the customer is the **trade receivable** (often called **receivables**) who agrees to pay an invoice at a future date.

When a purchase is made, the supplier is the **trade payable** (often called **payables**) who will be paid at a future date.

3.2 Capital and revenue transactions

Capital expenditure results in a non-current asset (such as plant and machinery) on the statement of financial position of the business. It results in acquiring an asset where the benefit continues over a long period of time, rather than being exhausted in a short period.

Revenue expenditure results in an expense in the statement of profit or loss account. Revenue expenses are shorter term expenses required to meet the ongoing operational costs of running a business. They are also known as operating expenses.

Activity 3: Revenue or capital expenditure

Required

Classify the following transactions as revenue or capital expenditure. Tick the correct box in the table below.

Transaction	Capital	Revenue
Purchase of building for £1m		
Purchase of goods for resale £50,000		
Payment of wages £25,000		
Purchase of materials for £75,000 to manufacture goods for resale		
Purchase of van for £15,000		

4 Recording transactions

Most businesses will have an accounting system that is based upon double entry bookkeeping methods. These are considered in detail in other units. In general terms the accounting system must be able to record each transaction (such as sales and purchases) and categorise each one correctly.

4.1 Manual and computerised accounting systems

The accounting system may be manual or computerised, or it may be a mixture of the two.

Manual systems are accounting records which are handwritten by the bookkeeper/accounting staff.

Advantages of a computerised accounting system:

- Errors are considerably reduced but not eliminated.

- Repetitive tasks like totalling and balancing off the accounts are automated and performed at the click of a button.

- Accounting data can be analysed in various formats and the system can produce financial statements.

Most of the material in this unit will be assessed based on a manual system as this is the best method of testing your competence.

4.2 Financial statements

The purpose of accounting is to record and classify the transactions of the business accurately. This allows financial statements for the business to be drawn up. For a company, financial statements in compliance with accounting standards are required by company law, but sole traders and partnerships also usually draw them up in order to assess the success and management of the business.

The two main financial statements are the statement of profit or loss and the statement of financial position. Although the preparation of these statements is not covered in Level 2 AAT studies, we will look briefly at them now to gain a better insight into the nature of the two key types of accounting: **financial accounting** and cost accounting.

4.2.1 Statement of profit or loss

Income less Expenses = Profit or Loss

The statement of profit or loss summarises all of the income of the business and deducts all the expenses. The expenses will include the cost of goods that have been purchased for resale, the cost of making any goods for sale, the costs of employing any staff and all the other everyday costs of running the business.

If the income is greater than the expenses a profit has been made, but if expenses exceed income then a loss has occurred.

4.2.2 Statement of financial position

The statement of financial position is a list of the monetary values of all the assets, **liabilities** and capital of the business on the last day of the accounting period. Assets are amounts that the business owns and liabilities are amounts that the business owes.

5 Financial accounting and cost accounting

A business's accounting system comprises three parts: its **bookkeeping system**, financial accounting and cost accounting (sometimes called **management accounting**).

The bookkeeping system records the business's past transactions and provides the information necessary for the other parts of the system. Note that most costs are stated at the historic cost, meaning the original cost at the time of the transaction.

5.1 Financial accounting

Financial accounting takes this information and processes it to prepare financial statements, such as the statement of profit or loss and the statement of financial position, for external publication at the end of each accounting period, normally a year. These are used by:

- Investors of money in the business, to assess its profitability and the level of drawings and dividends received

- Lenders and other suppliers of credit to the business (trade payables) to assess whether they will get paid

- Tax authorities (HMRC) to use as the basis for calculating the tax due on the profits of the business

Financial accounting has an external focus, involved in reporting accounting and other information to those outside the business such as investors, lenders and the regulatory authorities.

In the financial statements the business's costs incurred in the past are classified by their function, that is, production, selling and distribution, administration, and finance. We explain more about cost classification in a later chapter.

5.2 Cost accounting and management accounting

Originally cost accounting dealt with ways of accumulating historic costs and charging these costs to units of output or departments, in order to value inventory and establish profits. It has since been extended into planning, control and decision making. The terms cost accounting and management accounting are now used interchangeably.

(a) **Planning.** For example, the provision of forecast costs at different output levels

(b) **Control.** Such as the provision of actual and budget costs for comparison purposes

(c) **Decision making.** For example, the provision of information about actual unit costs for the period for pricing decisions

Cost accounting takes the same information as financial accounting and uses it to provide people inside the business with regular and focused financial information in order to run the business efficiently today and into the future. Cost accounting can analyse past costs incurred by element to determine how much it will cost in future to produce any unit of product, broken down into materials, labour and expenses or overheads. Cost accounting collects similar costs together so that they can be further analysed and used internally.

Unlike financial accounting, cost accounting has an internal focus, involved in reporting accounting and other information to those inside the business such as managers.

Cost accounts	Financial accounts
Cost accounts are used to aid management record, plan and control the organisation's activities and to help the decision-making process.	Financial accounts detail the performance of an organisation over a defined period and the state of affairs at the end of that period.
There is no legal requirement to prepare cost accounts.	In many countries (including the UK), limited companies must, by law, prepare financial accounts.

Cost accounts	Financial accounts
The format of cost accounts is entirely at management discretion: no strict rules govern the way they are prepared or presented. Each organisation can devise its own cost accounting system and format of reports.	The format of published financial accounts is determined by law (mainly the Companies Acts), by Statements of Standard Accounting Practice and by Financial Reporting Standards. In principle the accounts of different organisations can therefore be easily compared.
Cost accounts can focus on specific areas of an organisation's activities. Information may be produced to aid a decision rather than to be an end product of a decision.	Financial accounts concentrate on the business as a whole, aggregating revenues and costs from different operations, and are an end in themselves.
Cost accounts incorporate non-monetary measures. Management may need to know, for example, tonnes of aluminium produced, monthly machine hours or miles travelled by sales representatives.	Most financial accounting information is of a monetary nature.
Cost accounts are both a historical record and a future planning tool.	Financial accounts present an essentially historical picture of past operations.

Assessment focus point

An assessment question may give you a list of characteristics and ask you to indicate whether they relate to financial accounting or cost accounting.

Activity 4: Financial and cost accounting

The table below lists some of the characteristics of financial accounting and cost accounting.

Required

Indicate the characteristics for each system by putting a tick in the relevant column in the table below.

Characteristic	Financial accounting	Cost accounting
This system produces annual financial statements		
The statements from this system are used to estimate the cost of producing a product or providing a service		
The statements from this system are used to assist management in planning, control and decision making		
This system produces statements for external users		

Chapter summary

- There are three main types of business – a sole trader, a partnership or a limited company.

- Many transactions are undertaken by a business and these can be categorised as cash or credit transactions and as capital or revenue transactions.

- Different types of business will have predominantly different types of transactions – the types of industry that you may have to deal with are manufacturing, retail and service organisations.

- Accounting systems can be manual or computerised or a combination of the two.

- Management has three main roles in an organisation – decision making, planning and control. Relevant, up to date information is required in order to carry out these roles.

- Planning is both long range and short range – plans for the next year are set out in budgets which can be in terms of physical resources that are expected to be required, and in financial terms.

- Control is where the actual results of the business are compared to the budgeted figures and significant variances (differences) are reported to management.

- Financial accounting uses the information recorded by the bookkeeping system to produce financial statements and other reports for people external to the business.

- Management accounting uses some of the same information as financial accounting to provide information for people internal to the business, namely its managers in planning, decision making and controlling activities.

Keywords

- **Asset:** Something valuable that the business owns

- **Bookkeeping system:** The recording of the business's transactions in the general and subsidiary ledgers

- **Capital:** Amount that the business owes its owner once liabilities are deducted from assets

- **Capital transactions:** Purchases of assets for long-term use in the business, and gains from sales of these assets.

- **Cash transactions:** Transactions whereby payment or receipt is immediate

- **Credit transactions:** Transactions whereby payment or receipt is to be made at some future date

- **Financial accounting:** The use of information recorded by the bookkeeping system to prepare financial statements related to past transactions for external use: the statement of profit or loss and the statement of financial position

- **Liabilities:** Amounts that the business owes

- **Limited company:** A business that is owned by the shareholders and run by the directors – the owners have limited liability

- **Management accounting:** The use of both information on past performance and estimates of future activities to provide useful information for internal use by management in running the business today and into the future

- **Manufacturing organisation:** A business that makes the goods that it is to sell

- **Partnership:** A business run by a number of individuals trading together with the intention of making a profit

- **Payable:** Someone to whom the business owes money

- **Receivable:** Someone who owes money to the business

- **Retail organisation:** A business that buys in ready-made goods in order to sell them to customers

- **Revenue transactions:** All day-to-day revenue and expenses other than capital transactions

- **Service organisation:** A business that provides a service rather than a physical product

- **Sole trader:** A business that is owned and run by an individual

- **Statement of financial position:** Financial accounting statement showing the assets, liabilities and capital of the business on a particular date

- **Statement of profit or loss:** Financial accounting statement showing sales revenue plus other operating income less expenses equalling a profit or a loss

Test your learning

1   **For each of the following transactions indicate whether it should be classified as a cash or credit transaction. Tick the correct box.**

Transaction	Cash	Credit
Purchase of a van with payment agreed in one month		
Sale of goods paid for by credit card		
Purchase of printer paper accompanied by an invoice		
Sale of goods paid for by cheque		
Purchase of printer paper by cheque		

2   **For each of the following transactions indicate whether it should be classified as a capital or revenue transaction. Tick the correct box.**

Transaction	Capital	Revenue
Purchase of a computer for resale to a customer by a computer retailer		
Purchase of a computer by a computer retailer for use in the sales office		
Payment of wages by an accounting firm		
Purchase of a building by a property developer to serve as head office		

3   **In the table below, tick three items that would appear in a statement of profit or loss and two that would appear in a statement of financial position.**

	Statement of profit or loss	Statement of financial position
Sales revenue		
Non-current assets		
Expenses		
Current assets		
Profit or loss		

4   The table below lists some of the characteristics of financial accounting and cost accounting.

Required

Indicate two characteristics for each type of accounting by putting a tick in the relevant column of the table below.

Characteristic	Financial accounting	Cost accounting
It helps with decision making inside the business		
Its end product consists of statements for external publication		
It focuses on costs		
It focuses on asset valuations		

Cost classification

2

Learning outcomes

1.1	**Recognise how costs are collected and classified in different types of organisation**
	• How costs are collected in different organisations
	• What constitutes cost in different organisations and different types of organisation
	• How elements of cost are classified: labour, material, overhead
	• How costs are classified by nature: direct, indirect
1.2	**Recognise common costing techniques used in an organisation**
	• How product cost is determined: material, labour and overhead
1.3	**Identify the relationship between the costing and financial accounting systems within an organisation**
	• How each system uses cost: costing using many classifications of cost, financial accounting depending on historic cost
1.5	**Distinguish between cost, profit and investment centres**
	• Differences between cost centre, profit centre and investment centres
	• Use of different centres in different organisations
1.6	**Identify how materials, labour and overheads are classified and recorded**
	• How costs are classified: element, nature, behaviour, function

Assessment context

Cost classification is one of the key areas of the syllabus and, as well as providing you with key terminology for many of the following chapters, is very examinable.

Qualification context

This section includes terminology that will be used throughout this unit and also in Level 3 of the AAT qualification.

Business context

Grouping costs together is essential for a business to be able to analyse costs, create budgets and plan effectively.

Chapter overview

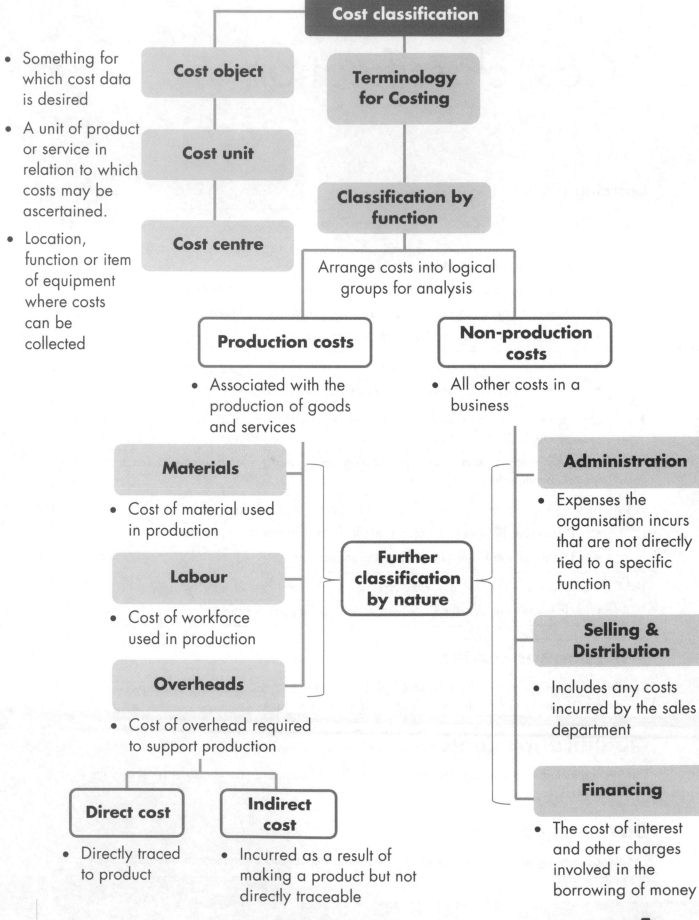

Cost classification

Cost object

- Something for which cost data is desired

Cost unit

- A unit of product or service in relation to which costs may be ascertained.

Cost centre

- Location, function or item of equipment where costs can be collected

Terminology for Costing

Classification by function

Arrange costs into logical groups for analysis

Production costs

- Associated with the production of goods and services

Non-production costs

- All other costs in a business

Materials

- Cost of material used in production

Labour

- Cost of workforce used in production

Overheads

- Cost of overhead required to support production

Further classification by nature

Administration

- Expenses the organisation incurs that are not directly tied to a specific function

Selling & Distribution

- Includes any costs incurred by the sales department

Financing

- The cost of interest and other charges involved in the borrowing of money

Direct cost

- Directly traced to product

Indirect cost

- Incurred as a result of making a product but not directly traceable

Introduction

In the bookkeeping system costs are classified into their ledger accounts as:

- Purchases
- Wages
- Various expenses – rent, telephone, electricity etc

Financial accounting and management accounting take a slightly more complicated view of costs.

Financial accounting classification of costs

In financial accounting the most important classification of costs is into **capital expenditure** (on non-current assets) and **revenue expenditure**.

Non-current assets are assets that are used in the business for more than one accounting period to provide benefits over time, rather than being bought to make profit on their resale in just one period. Capital expenditure therefore includes the cost of plant and machinery, land and buildings, office equipment and motor vehicles. These benefits are (we hope!) the profits earned from using the assets in the business.

Revenue expenditure includes:

- The purchase of materials for manufacture and goods for resale
- The cost of maintaining or servicing non-current assets
- The costs of running the business, including wages

Management accounting classification of costs

In management accounting the classification of costs needs to be more detailed and focused, so managers can use it to plan, make decisions and control operations. It is also more flexible.

Generally speaking, management accounting is concerned with revenue expenditure, although in some cases it includes amounts that represent how much of a non-current asset is 'used up' in a period (called depreciation).

Costs can be classified by function, such as whether they are incurred in production or by the administration department. A further basic classification of costs is between the **elements of cost**: materials, labour and **expenses**. Finally they can be classified by their nature. That is, by whether they are incurred directly in the course of making a product or providing a service (**direct costs**) or indirectly in providing general management, selling, finance or administrative support (**indirect costs**).

Remember: How costs are classified depends on how the information on costs is to be used.

1 Some cost accounting concepts

A **cost object** is anything for which cost data is desired, for example products, product lines, jobs, customers, or departments and divisions of a company.

A **cost unit** is a unit of product or service in relation to which costs may be ascertained. The cost unit should be appropriate to the type of business. For example:

Business	Appropriate cost unit
Car manufacturer	Car
Builder	Job/Contract
Management consultant	Project

A **cost centre** is a location, function or item of equipment in respect of which costs may be ascertained and related to cost units for control purposes.

Each cost centre acts as a 'collecting place' for certain costs before they are analysed further. We will come back to cost centres later in the chapter.

2 Cost classification

2.1 Classification by function

As we explained in the introduction, within a business, costs are often classified into logical groups. Classification by function involves relating the costs to the activities causing the costs. For example:

(a) Production or manufacturing cost
(b) Administration costs
(c) Marketing or selling and distribution costs
(d) Finance costs

In practice the distinction between these functions is not always clear, particularly when we are talking about administration costs, as there are no rules or regulations to follow, just common sense. What is more, these are not the only possible functions within a business. Large companies often have a research and development function, or a training function. It depends on the type of business. Some examples of costs by function are given in the following table:

Function	Ledger account
Production costs	Materials used in making a product
	Wages of employees making a product
	Electricity incurred to operate machines used in making a product

Function	Ledger account
Selling and distribution costs	Advertising Delivery costs to customers Sales staff salaries
Administration costs	Secretarial and accounting costs General management salaries Rent of office buildings
Finance costs	Interest on a loan or overdraft Fees for arranging a loan

The total costs of running a manufacturing business are often classified in the following way:

	£
Materials	X
Labour	X
Expenses	X
Total production costs	X
Non-production costs	
Administration costs	X
Selling and distribution costs	X
Financing costs	X
TOTAL COSTS	X

Examples of non-production costs include accountant's salary, office rent, non-manufacturing materials (known as consumables, eg stationery) and services (eg solicitors' fees paid).

Activity 1: Classification by function

A company manufactures and sells toys and incurs the following costs.

Required

Classify the following costs by function (production, administration, selling and distribution, and financing costs) by putting a tick in the relevant column of the table below.

	Production costs	Administration costs	Selling and distribution	Financing costs
Purchase of plastic and rubber material				
Rental of finished goods warehouse				
Depreciation of its own fleet of delivery vehicles				
Commission paid to sales staff				
Insurance of office furniture				
Interest paid on loan				

2.2 Classification by element

A different way of classifying revenue expenses looks at the three major cost elements: materials, labour and expenses (also referred to as **overheads**: the two terms are used interchangeably in this unit).

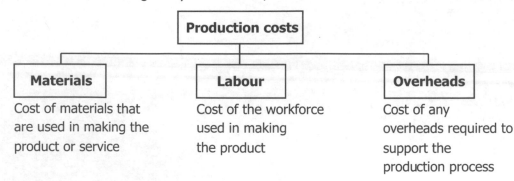

Production costs

Materials
Cost of materials that are used in making the product or service

Labour
Cost of the workforce used in making the product

Overheads
Cost of any overheads required to support the production process

Illustration 1 Classification by element

Mabley Ltd makes picnic baskets in its factory. It fills these with sandwich boxes and vacuum flasks which it purchases ready-made from a supplier, then sells the completed product to retailers.

Mabley Ltd can use management accounting to classify the transactions in its ledger accounts by elements as follows:

Element	Ledger accounts
Materials	Materials used in making baskets
	Cost of items purchased to fill the baskets
	Machine lubricants and spare parts
Labour	Wages of employees making the baskets
	Wages of employees supervising the production workforce
	Sales staff salaries
	General management salaries
Expenses or overheads	Advertising
	Delivery costs to customers
	Secretarial and accounting costs
	Rent of office buildings
	Interest on a loan or overdraft
	Fees for arranging a loan

Activity 2: Classification by element

Cellophane Ltd produces packaging for toys.

Required

Classify the following costs by element (material, labour or overhead) by putting a tick in the relevant column of the table below.

Cost	Material	Labour	Overhead
Insurance of factory			
Plastic used in the production of packaging			
Wages paid to employees			
Rent of office space			
Training course for factory workers			

Assessment focus point

An assessment question may give you a list of costs and ask you to categorise them by their function or element.

2.3 Classification by nature

Each element (materials, labour, overhead) can be subdivided into

Direct costs are costs that can be directly identified with a particular unit of production or service provided

Indirect costs are costs that cannot be directly identified with a unit of production or service.

It is usually easy to identify the amount of a direct expense that is spent on one unit, but it is more difficult to do so with indirect costs as they are not spent directly on one unit. They are usually spent in relation to a number of units.

Here are some examples:

Direct materials	Materials that are incorporated into the finished product (eg wood used in the construction of a table).
Indirect materials	Materials that are used in the production process but not incorporated into the product (eg machine lubricants and spare parts). Insignificant costs that are attributable to each unit are sometimes included in indirect materials for convenience (eg nails and glue).
Direct labour	Wages paid to those workers who make products in a manufacturing business (eg machine operators) or perform the service in a service business (eg hairdressers in a hair salon).
Indirect labour	Wages and salaries of the other staff, such as supervisors, storekeepers and maintenance workers.
Direct expenses	Expenses that are identifiable with each unit of production, such as patent royalties payable to the inventor of a new product or process.
Indirect expenses	Expenses that are not spent on individual units of production (eg rent and rates, electricity and telephone).

In costing, the three types of direct cost are often lumped together and called **prime cost**.

Prime cost = Direct materials + Direct labour + Direct expenses

The three types of indirect cost are often lumped together and called overheads.

Overheads = Indirect materials + Indirect labour + Indirect expenses

Assessment focus point

An assessment question may give you a list of costs and ask you to indicate whether they are classed as direct or indirect costs.

3 Responsibility centres

A manufacturing business is likely to split naturally into a variety of different areas or departments. Typical examples may be:

- Cutting
- Assembling
- Finishing
- Packing
- Warehouse
- Stores
- Maintenance
- Administration
- Selling and distribution
- Finance

The precise split of a business will depend upon its nature and the nature of its activities and transactions. However the business is split, managers need to know the costs and/or income of each department to be able to make decisions, plan operations and control the business.

3.1 Cost, profit and investment centres

Responsibility centres are areas of the business for which costs or revenues are gathered and compared to budgets for control purposes. There are different types of responsibility centre (cost, profit and **investment centre**) depending on the type of cost and/or revenue that the centre deals with.

The name 'responsibility centre' comes from the fact that each area of the business (each responsibility centre) has a manager who is responsible for the activities of that area.

3.2 Cost centres

Each area or department which incurs costs only is known as a cost centre.

Key term

Cost centre is a location, function or item of equipment in respect of which costs may be ascertained and related to cost units for control purposes.

Each cost centre acts as a 'collecting place' for certain costs before they are analysed further. A cost centre manager is accountable for costs only.

Notes

1   Cost centres may be set up in any way the business thinks appropriate.

2   Usually, only manufacturing costs are considered, and hence we will focus on factory cost centres.

3.2.1 Service and production cost centres

- **Production cost centres**. These are factory cost centres through which units of production actually flow.

- **Service cost centres**. These support or service the production cost centres.

3.3 Profit centres

Some organisations work on a **profit centre** basis. A profit centre is similar to a cost centre but is accountable for both costs and revenue. Commonly, several cost centres will together make up one profit centre.

Illustration 2 Profit centres

In a retail business, each individual shop produces income as well as incurring costs. Both costs and income for each shop are gathered together so each one is a profit centre. When the income and the costs are compared the final result will be the profit or loss made by the profit centre.

3.4 Investment centres

Divisions in an organisation may be investment centres. An investment centre is accountable for costs, revenues and investments in assets. So it incorporates the features of a cost and a profit centre.

Chapter summary

- For management accounting purposes, costs can be classified into the elements of materials, labour and expenses, or by function (production, selling and distribution, administration, and finance) or by nature (direct or indirect).

- The name 'responsibility centre' comes from the fact that each area of the business (each responsibility centre) has a manager who is responsible for the activities of that area.

  - Cost centre managers are responsible for costs only

  - Profit centre managers are responsible for costs and revenues only

  - Investment centre managers are responsible for costs, revenues and capital expenditure

Keywords

- **Cost centre:** An area of the business for which costs are collected together for management accounting purposes. A cost centre manager is accountable for costs only.

- **Cost object:** Anything for which cost data is desired, for example products, product lines, jobs, customers or departments and divisions of a company.

- **Cost unit:** A unit of product or service in relation to which costs are ascertained

- **Direct costs:** These can be directly identified with making a product or providing a service

- **Elements of cost:** Classifying costs into materials, labour and expenses/overheads

- **Expenses:** Costs incurred by the business that do not relate to materials or labour

- **Indirect costs:** These cannot be directly identified with making a product or providing a service

- **Investment centre:** A profit centre with additional responsibilities for capital investment

- **Overheads:** A term used synonymously with 'expenses'

- **Prime cost:** Direct material + direct labour + direct expenses

- **Profit centre:** Similar to a cost centre but the manager is responsible for both revenues and costs

- **Responsibility centre:** A department or function whose performance is the direct responsibility of a specific manager

- **Revenue expenditure:** Includes the purchase of materials for manufacture and goods for resale plus expenses incurred in the business

Test your learning

1   **For a manufacturer of washing machines, classify the following costs by element (materials, labour or overheads) by putting a tick in the relevant column of the table below.**

Cost	Materials	Labour	Overheads
Metal used for casing			
Business rates on warehouse			
Wages of operatives in assembly department			
Salary of factory supervisor			

2   **For a contract cleaning business, classify the following costs by nature (direct or indirect) by putting a tick in the relevant column of the table below.**

Cost	Direct	Indirect
Detergent used for cleaning floors		
Depreciation of vacuum cleaner		
Wages of bookings assistant		
Wages of cleaners		

3   **For a manufacturer of bricks, classify the following costs by function (production, administration, or selling and distribution) by putting a tick in the relevant column of the table below.**

Cost	Production	Selling and distribution	Administration
Purchases of sand			
Fuel for salesperson's vehicle			
Printer paper for office			
Wages of factory workers			

4   **Look at the list of costs below and decide whether each one would be classified as a production cost, a selling and distribution cost or an administration cost. Put a tick in the correct box.**

Cost	Production	Selling and distribution	Administration
Factory rent			
Managing Director's salary			
Sales Director's salary			
Depreciation charge on office equipment			
Depreciation charge on factory plant and equipment			
Fuel for delivery vans			
Factory heating and lighting			

5   A manager has control of the costs, revenues and assets of their division.

Required

What type of responsibility centre is this?

	Tick
Cost centre	
Profit centre	
Investment centre	

Coding costs

3

Learning outcome

1.6	Identify how materials, labour and overheads are classified and recorded
	• How costs are coded using numeric, alphabetic and alphanumeric coding systems

Assessment context

Expect to see questions where you have to set up appropriate codes for different types of income and expenditure incurred by cost centres and profit centres.

Qualification context

Coding income and expenditure from invoices and payroll information helps with the accurate collection of costs, which are then used for further analysis.

Business context

Most businesses use computerised accounting systems where coding of income and expenditure correctly from raw data, is of paramount importance.

Chapter overview

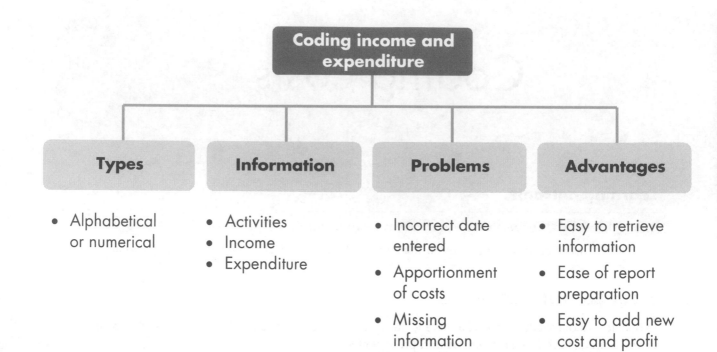

Coding income and expenditure

Types
- Alphabetical or numerical

Information
- Activities
- Income
- Expenditure

Problems
- Incorrect date entered
- Apportionment of costs
- Missing information

Advantages
- Easy to retrieve information
- Ease of report preparation
- Easy to add new cost and profit centres

Introduction

In the previous chapter we explained how costs can be classified in different ways and how they can be collected in cost centres, profit centres and investment centres. Now we will see how coding invoices, payroll information and other information ensures the accurate collection of costs and other data.

1 Methods of coding

Businesses want revenue and costs incurred to be charged to the correct responsibility centre. In order for this to happen the revenue or expenditure must be coded to show what type it is and which responsibility centre it is to be charged to.

A code is a system of words, letters, figures or symbols used to help with classification of items. Codes are commonly used for entering information into computer systems.

Each business will have its own coding structure. Here we consider various methods of coding:

(a)   Alphabetic coding systems
(b)   Numeric coding systems
(c)   Alpha-numeric coding systems

In general terms, most businesses arrange their ledger accounts into groups representing the different accounting aspects of the business. For example, the groups of accounts that may be required might be:

- Income accounts
- Expense accounts
- Asset accounts
- Liability accounts
- Capital accounts

1.1 Numeric coding

A **numeric coding** system is where the code is entirely numerical. For example, the general ledger codes might be set up as follows:

Income accounts   0001–0199
Expenses accounts   0200–0499
Asset accounts   0500–0699
Liability accounts   0700–0899
Capital accounts   0900–1000

There are potentially 1,000 ledger accounts here. They do not all have to be used, but the coding system must be flexible enough to allow for new accounts to be opened up.

1.2 Alpha-numeric coding

An **alpha-numeric coding** system uses a mixture of letters and numbers to code the ledger accounts. For example, the general ledger account codes might be set up as:

Income accounts	A001–200
Expenses accounts	B001–200
Asset accounts	C001–200
Liability accounts	D001–200
Capital accounts	E001–200

1.3 Alphabetic coding

An **alphabetic coding** system uses just letters to code the ledger accounts. For example, the general ledger account codes might be set up as:

Income accounts	AAA–DZZ
Expenses accounts	EAA–JZZ
Asset accounts	KAA–PZZ
Liability accounts	QAA–VZZ
Capital accounts	WAA–ZZZ

2 Coding the elements

A coding list for accounting transactions should be designed so that it is possible to collect and produce information for both management and financial accounting purposes. This helps to avoid the need to enter the same information into the computer more than once.

Costs incurred by a business should be analysed into materials, labour or expenses and coded to the correct cost centre.

2.1 Materials

The net amount of each purchase invoice that arrives must be analysed to determine the type of cost and the cost centre to which it should be charged. Each element of the invoice must then be coded to ensure that the cost is collected for the correct cost centre. Note that the cost centre may also be a profit centre, in which case income would also be coded to it, or an investment centre, in which case assets, liabilities and capital may also be coded to it. For the moment, however, we shall just use the term cost centre for simplicity.

Illustration 1 Coding materials

Wilmshurst Furniture Makers has three cost centres and a management accounting coding system that uses a six-digit code. All cost centre codes begin with the digits 01. The second two digits in the code then denote the precise cost centre to which the expense relates, as follows:

- Cutting cost centre   01
- Assembly cost centre   02
- Polishing cost centre   03

The final two digits represent the type of cost:

- Materials   01
- Labour   02
- Expenses   03

We will now code each element of cost to show the type of cost – materials – and the cost centre to which they relate.

INVOICE

J.J. Supplies
Park Road
Benham DR6 2PQ
Tel 0303413 Fax 0303414
VAT Reg 0611 3987 24

To: Wilmshurst Furniture
Makers
Industrial Estate
Benham
DR6 2FF

Invoice number: 361120

Date/tax point: 29 Dec 20X6

Order number: PO 49681

Account number: W49

Quantity	Description	Stock code	Unit amount £	Total £
20m	Solid oak panel 40cm	41992	30.20 per m.	010101 604.00
2 Litres	Beeswax polish	73126	22.00 per litre	010301 44.00
		Net total		648.00
		VAT		129.60
		Invoice total		777.60

Terms
Net 30 days
E & OE

The solid oak panel is coded as follows:

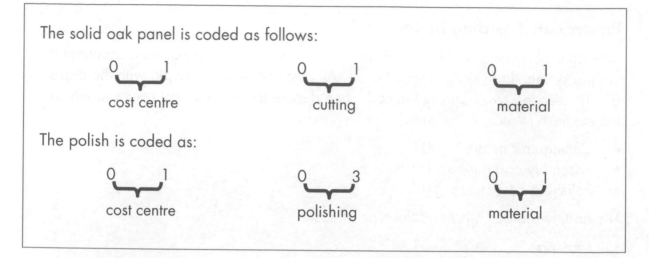

The polish is coded as:

2.2 Labour

Labour costs must also be coded. Note that some elements of the cost of employing people – such as national insurance contributions (NIC) – may be charged as an expense/overhead (an indirect cost) rather than as labour.

Illustration 2 Coding labour costs

Wilmshurst's policy is to charge basic and overtime hours as labour, and employer's NIC as an expense/overhead.

In Week 39 Jim worked for 29 hours in the cutting department (including 6 hours of overtime) and 12 hours in the assembly department for £378.40 in total (41 hours in total). The employer's NIC is calculated as £36.02 in total.

```
His pay is analysed as follows:
                                                          £
Cutting cost centre  - labour 23 hours @ £8.60        197.80
Cutting cost centre  - labour 6 hours @ £12.90         77.40
Cutting cost centre  - expense NIC £36.02 ×            25.48
29/41
Assembly cost centre - labour 12 hours @ £8.60        103.20
Assembly cost centre - expense NIC £36.02 ×            10.54
12/41
Total cost (£378.40 + £36.02)                         414.42
```

```
This must now be coded:
                                      £        Code
Cutting cost centre  - labour       275.20    010102
(197.80 + 77.40)
Cutting cost centre  - expense (NIC)  25.48    010103
Assembly cost centre - labour        103.20    010202
Assembly cost centre - expense (NIC)  10.54    010203
```

The first two digits are always 01 as these are cost centres. The second pair of digits are 01 for cutting and 02 for assembly. The final digits are 02 for the labour element and 03 for the expense element.

2.3 Expenses

Expense (or overhead) costs must also be coded.

Illustration 3 Coding expenses

Wilmshurst's factory rent and power costs were apportioned to the three production cost centres and must now be coded:

	£	Code
Factory rent		
Cutting	3,000	010103
Assembly	2,000	010203
Polishing	1,000	010303
Factory power		
Cutting	1,320	010103
Assembly	330	010203
Polishing	550	010303

The first two digits are 01 as these are cost centres. The second two digits represent the cost centre itself. The final two digits, 03, show that these are expenses.

2.4 Sales income

So far we have only concerned ourselves with costs. However, sales income or revenue must also be recognised in the management accounting records if the business operates profit centres (and/or investment centres). This is done by analysing the sales invoices to the correct profit centre and coding them appropriately.

Illustration 4 Sales income

Wilmshurst makes its sales through three outlets, in Dopham, Nutley and Jenson. The coding for sales is as follows:

First two digits	02 represents a profit centre	
Second two digits	Dopham profit centre	10
	Nutley profit centre	11
	Jenson profit centre	12
Third two digits	This depends upon the type of sale	
	– 5ft dining table	11
	– 6ft dining table	12
	– Round coffee table	13
	– Square coffee table	14
	– Dining chair	15
	– 2-drawer chest	16
	– 3-drawer chest	17
	– 5ft wardrobe	18
	– 6ft wardrobe	19

BPP LEARNING MEDIA

Given below are two sales invoices that have been coded.

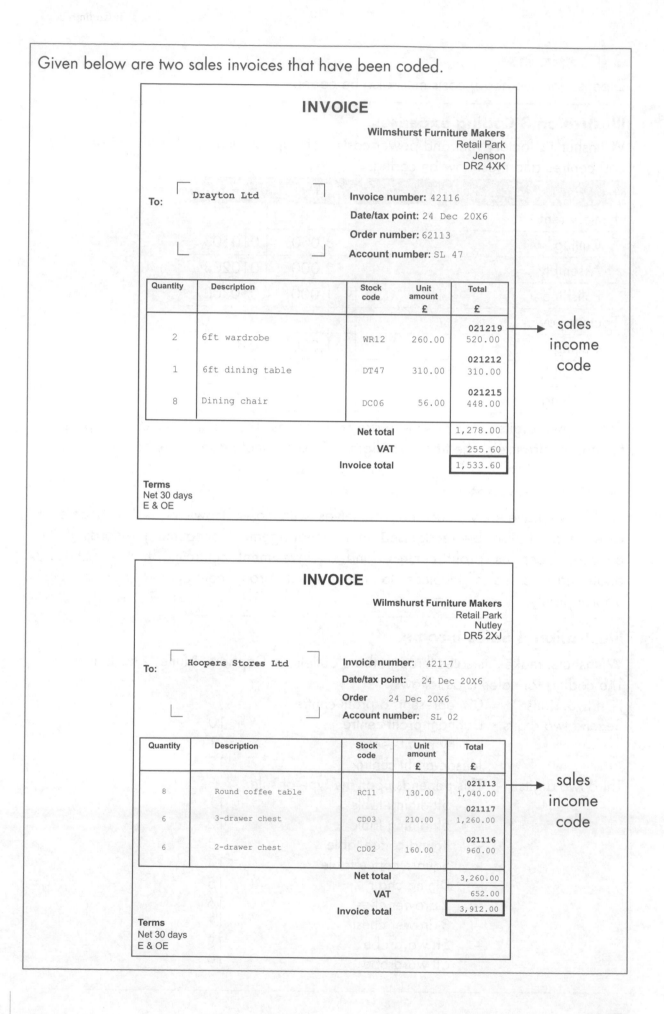

INVOICE

Wilmshurst Furniture Makers
Retail Park
Jenson
DR2 4XK

To: ⌐ Drayton Ltd ¬

Invoice number: 42116

Date/tax point: 24 Dec 20X6

Order number: 62113

Account number: SL 47

Quantity	Description	Stock code	Unit amount £	Total £
2	6ft wardrobe	WR12	260.00	**021219** 520.00
1	6ft dining table	DT47	310.00	**021212** 310.00
8	Dining chair	DC06	56.00	**021215** 448.00
			Net total	1,278.00
			VAT	255.60
			Invoice total	1,533.60

→ sales income code

Terms
Net 30 days
E & OE

INVOICE

Wilmshurst Furniture Makers
Retail Park
Nutley
DR5 2XJ

To: ⌐ Hoopers Stores Ltd ¬

Invoice number: 42117

Date/tax point: 24 Dec 20X6

Order 24 Dec 20X6

Account number: SL 02

Quantity	Description	Stock code	Unit amount £	Total £
8	Round coffee table	RC11	130.00	**021113** 1,040.00
6	3-drawer chest	CD03	210.00	**021117** 1,260.00
6	2-drawer chest	CD02	160.00	**021116** 960.00
			Net total	3,260.00
			VAT	652.00
			Invoice total	3,912.00

→ sales income code

Terms
Net 30 days
E & OE

The coding of each item is:

6ft wardrobe	0 2	1 2	1 9
	profit centre	Jenson	6ft wardrobe
6ft dining table	0 2	1 2	1 2
	profit centre	Jenson	6ft dining table
Dining chair	0 2	1 2	1 5
	profit centre	Jenson	dining chair
Round coffee table	0 2	1 1	1 3
	profit centre	Nutley	round coffee table
3-drawer chest	0 2	1 1	1 7
	profit centre	Nutley	3-drawer chest
2-drawer chest	0 2	1 1	1 6
	profit centre	Nutley	2-drawer chest

3 Benefits and problems of coding

3.1 Benefits of coding

A coding system can:

- Record and retrieve information quickly and easily
- Be automatically accurate and have built-in checking facilities
- Be capable of sorting information in many different ways and printing off detailed reports as required

3.2 Problems with coding

Management information reports should make apparent any significant items of income and expenditure which have been coded incorrectly. For example, if sales in one month are ten times their usual size it is likely to be due to a coding error.

A significant problem with coding is the potential to enter the data incorrectly into the computer system.

Problems with coding can also arise as some costs relate to more than one cost centre. For example, one electricity bill may be received for the electricity used by all the departments in the company. In this situation, the electricity cost needs to be apportioned across all the departments on a basis that reflects, as fairly as possible, how much electricity each department has used.

Other people may need to help with coding transactions, providing missing information and correcting errors.

Activity 1: Coding of costs

You have just started a new job as an accountant for Medieval Castle, a business which splits its activities into four main profit centres with the following code prefixes.

T: Guided tours
C: Café
R: Retail shops
G: Garden walks

For costs which relate to all four profit centres the prefix X is used; these costs are allocated between the profit centres at a later date.

The above prefixes are followed by a numerical code, which describes the type of revenue or expense involved. The numerical codes are summarised as follows:

01   Phone and fax
02   Labour
03   Goods for resale
04   Heat and light
05   Staff clothing and equipment
06   Rental costs

Required

Complete the table by coding the following invoices so that they can be correctly entered onto the computer system. Each transaction should have a three-character code:

Nos	Invoices	Invoice £	Code
123	Retail staff salaries	20,000	
124	Costumes for tour guides	489	
125	Garden forks	150	
126	Electricity bill for Medieval Castle	3,598	
127	Rental of café building	1,843	
128	Retail shop telephone bill	317	
129	Gardening clothes for staff	271	
130	Miniature castles for resale	52	
131	Payroll costs	2,000	
132	Walking sticks for resale to walkers	229	
133	Tea, coffee and fresh cream cakes	99	

Activity 2: Coding transactions

Spelprint is a printing company. Lesley Dodds' responsibility is to code sales, purchase and payroll transactions. The appropriate codes on data input sheets are then used for entering the transactions onto Spelprint's computerised accounting system. You have been asked to code the transactions instead.

When doing the coding, refer to the extracts from the company's policy manual which follow. The purpose of the coding is to allocate costs and revenues to the appropriate cost and profit centres, and also to distinguish between different types of costs and revenues.

Policy manual (extracts)

Coding of expenditure

Each item of expenditure must be coded with two pieces of information:

- The cost centre (see below)
- The cost category (see below)

Cost centres and codes	
Direct production materials (including paper, card, ink)	810
Employee costs (comprising wages and salaries, including employer NIC)	820
Expenses (including services such as accountancy and advertising, and indirect materials such as lubricants)	830

Cost categories and codes	
Purchase of paper for printing jobs	910
Purchase of card for printing jobs	920
Purchase of ink for printing jobs	930
Gross wages and salaries	940
Employer NIC	950
Accountancy and legal costs	960
Purchase of lubricants	970
Advertising	980
Computer consumables	990

You find a data entry sheet prepared by your colleague Nisar Khan. Nisar has entered details of purchase invoices received yesterday, 8 January 20X0.

Required

Complete the following data entry sheet by entering the correct cost centre codes and cost category codes.

Data entry sheet: purchase invoices

Date 20X0	Supplier	Details of purchase	Amount £	Cost centre code	Cost category code
8 Jan	Acorn Mills Limited	Paper for printing jobs	971.50		
8 Jan	Thorn & Co	Accountancy services	275.00		
8 Jan	Parslow Limited	Lubricants	322.72		
8 Jan	Maxwell Smith	Ink for printing jobs	194.00		
8 Jan	Rimmer Limited	Paper for printing jobs	513.81		

Activity 3: Coding transactions continued

The following is a salaries summary for Spelprint for December 20X0.

Required

Enter the appropriate control totals and codes on the input sheet ready for inputting the payroll details to the accounts system.

Salaries summary for the month of December 20X0

Employee name	Gross pay £	PAYE tax £	Employee NIC £	Net pay £	Employer NIC £
Baldeesh Amar	1,280.00	217.00	101.66	961.34	122.50
Lesley Dodds	940.00	129.00	62.37	748.63	71.04
Deepak Elim	850.00	91.00	51.37	707.63	59.78
Jenny Fylde	2,200.00	413.00	199.65	1,587.35	232.32
Henry Maple	790.00	146.00	82.00	562.00	100.53
John Preston	2,800.00	550.00	243.55	2,006.45	309.12
Amy Saunders	1,100.00	157.00	78.65	864.35	91.52
Control total	**9,960.00**	**1,703.00**	**819.25**	**7,437.75**	**986.81**

Coding sheets: salaries for the month of December 20X0

| Description | Amount £ | Accounts code | |
		Cost centre	Cost category
Gross pay			
Employer NIC			

Activity 4: Investment centre coding

Crowngate Ltd has set up an investment centre for a project it is undertaking. The company uses an alpha numeric system for its investments, revenues and costs as outlined in the first **four** columns of the table below.

Required

Code the transactions listed in the transaction column of the table below using the code column for your answers. Each transaction should have a five-character code.

Activity	Code	Nature of cost	Sub-code	Transaction	Code
Investments	IN	External	200	Internal investment funds	
		Internal	220	Salaries of project staff	
Revenues	RE	UK	300	Overseas revenue arising from project	
		Overseas	330	Materials used on project	
Costs	CO	Material	400	Bank loan raised for investment in the project	
		Labour	500	Sales to UK customers	
		Overheads	600		

Assessment focus point

An assessment question may give you a list of transactions and ask you to code them.

Chapter summary

- There are many methods of coding, and each business will devise its own system.

- Numeric and alpha-numeric coding systems are the most common in practice and in assessments.

- Each purchase invoice is analysed and coded as to the type of cost (materials, labour or expense) and the cost centre (or profit or investment centre) that it relates to.

- The payroll details are also coded to indicate the elements of gross pay that are treated as labour and any element that is treated as an expense, as well as the cost centres etc they relate to.

- The expenses are coded to show the cost centre they relate to.

- Sales invoices are analysed to indicate the profit centre they relate to and in some systems also the product that is being sold.

- In some systems, assets, liabilities and capital can be coded for the investment centre to which they relate.

Keywords

- **Alphabetic coding:** A coding system that uses just letters
- **Alpha-numeric coding:** A coding system that uses letters and numbers
- **Numeric coding:** A coding system that uses numbers only

1   Pole Potteries has a three-digit coding system for its cost centres:

    Digit one   1   means that this is a cost centre

    Digit two   denotes the actual cost centre:

                1   throwing

                2   baking

                3   painting

                4   packaging

                5   stores

                6   maintenance

                7   selling and distribution

                8   canteen

                9   administration

    Digit three   denotes the type of cost:

                1   materials

                2   labour

                3   expenses

Required

Code the following purchase invoice using the three-digit coding system above. Enter your answers into the boxes on the invoices below.

INVOICE

Purbeck Clay
Granite Yard
Compston BH3 4TL
Tel 01929 4648410
VAT Reg 1164 2810 67

To: Pole Potteries

Invoice number: 36411

Date/tax point: 16 Dec 20X6

Order number: 11663

Account number: SL 42

Quantity	Description	Inventory code	Unit amount £	Total £
50 kg	Throwing clay	TC412	6.80	340.00
10 Litres	Paint – Fuchsia	PF67	2.80	28.00
			Net total	368.00
			VAT	73.60
			Invoice total	441.60

Terms
Net 30 days
E & OE

2   Lara Binns works for Pole Potteries. Her gross wage for Week 39 has been analysed so that the NIC can be treated as an expense as follows:

	£	Code
Throwing – labour (23 hours @ £9.60) + (3 hours @ £9.60 × 2)	278.40	
Baking – labour 15 hours @ £9.60	144.00	
Throwing – expense – employer's NIC	26.42	
Baking – expense – employer's NIC	15.25	

Required

Use the coding system in question 1 to code Lara's pay correctly, entering the code in the box next to each description in the table above.

3 The expenses of Pole Potteries for the period have been analysed and summarised below.

Required

Use the coding system to code these too.

	£	Code
Throwing – expense – rent £15,000 × 15%	2,250	
Throwing – expense – cleaning	200	
Throwing – total	2,450	
Baking – expense – rent £15,000 × 40%	6,000	
Baking – expense – servicing	600	
Baking – total	6,600	
Painting – expense – rent £15,000 × 15%	2,250	
Packaging – expense – rent £5,000 × 20%	1,000	
Stores – expense – rent £5,000 × 80%	4,000	
Maintenance – expense – rent £15,000 × 10%	1,500	
Selling and distribution – expense – rent £3,000 × 50%	1,500	
Selling and distribution – expense – advertising	400	
Selling and distribution – total	1,900	
Canteen – expense – rent £15,000 × 20%	3,000	
Administration – expense – rent £3,000 × 50%	1,500	

4 A manufacturer of washing machines uses a numerical coding structure based on one profit centre and three cost centres as outlined below. Each code has a sub-code, so each transaction will be coded in the format */** (eg 1/20).

Profit/Cost centre	Code	Sub-classification	Sub-code
Sales	1	UK sales	10
		EU sales	20
Production	2	Direct cost	10
		Indirect cost	20
Selling and distribution	3	Direct cost	10
		Indirect cost	20
Administration	4	Direct cost	10
		Indirect cost	20

Required

Code the following revenue and expense transactions that have been extracted from purchase invoices, sales invoices and the payroll, using the table below.

Transaction	Code
Materials for casings	
Sales to Paris, EU	
Business rates on factory	
Printing of marketing leaflets	
Sales to Holmfirth, UK	
Office stationery	

5   Herbert Ltd has set up an investment centre for a project it is undertaking over a period of years. It uses an alpha coding system for its investments, revenues and costs and then further classifies numerically as outlined in the columns of the table below.

Profit/Cost centre	Code	Nature of cost	Sub-code
Investments	INV	External	100
		Internal	200
Revenues	REV	UK	300
		Overseas	400
Costs	COS	Material	500
		Labour	600
		Overheads	700

Required

Code the following transactions using the table below. Each transaction should have a six character code.

Transaction	Code
Architect fees for project	
Herbert Ltd money invested in project	
Material used on project	
Project revenue arising in Africa	
Bank loan invested in project	
Salaries paid to employees	

Cost behaviour

Assessment context

A good understanding of cost behaviour is very important on this unit so ensure you complete all the activities on this area.

Qualification context

This section introduces concepts and terms that are fundamental for this unit as well as units at the next level.

Business context

Understanding cost behaviour helps businesses to ascertain accurate profitability, plan/budget better and make good business decisions.

Chapter overview

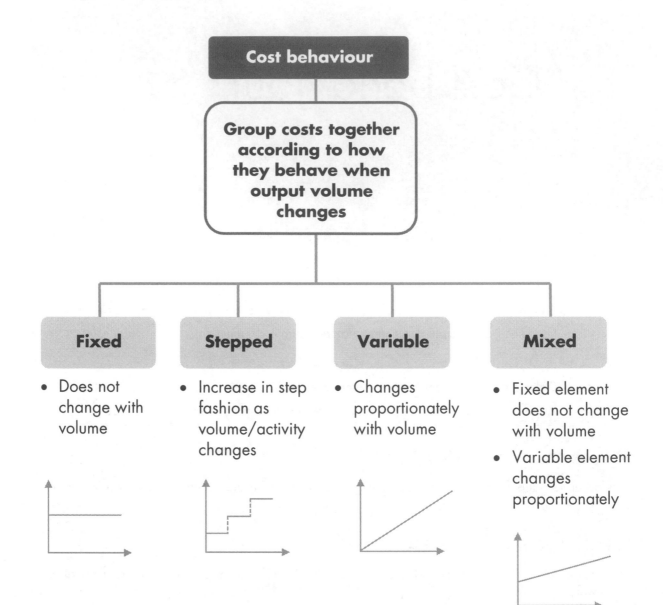

Cost behaviour

Group costs together according to how they behave when output volume changes

Fixed
- Does not change with volume

Stepped
- Increase in step fashion as volume/activity changes

Variable
- Changes proportionately with volume

Mixed
- Fixed element does not change with volume
- Variable element changes proportionately

Introduction

In Chapter 2 we considered how costs can be classified by function (production, administration etc). We also saw how costs can be split by element into materials, labour and expenses/overheads, and by nature between direct or indirect costs.

In this chapter we examine **cost behaviour**, that is, how a cost behaves in relation to activity levels.

A business needs to know how costs behave with output so that predictions of costs can be made.

1 Fixed, variable and semi-variable costs

1.1 Fixed cost

If activity changes and the total cost stays the same, the cost is classified as a fixed cost. Each unit of output causes no extra amount of cost to be incurred, so the cost per unit decreases the more units are produced, and increases if the number of units produced declines.

1.2 Variable cost

If activity changes and the total cost changes in exactly the same way, the cost is classified as a **variable cost**. This means that each unit of production causes the same amount of cost to be incurred, so the cost per unit is the same however many units are produced.

1.3 Semi-variable cost

If activity changes and the total cost changes but not in exactly the same way, the cost is classified as a **semi-variable cost** – there is an element of fixed cost and an element of variable cost. The cost per unit changes with the number of units produced, but not in a consistent manner.

> ### Illustration 1 Materials, labour and expenses
>
> Tilling Ltd makes tiles, incurring materials costs, labour costs and expenses.
>
> **Materials costs:**
>
> When 10,000 tiles are produced, total materials cost is £20,000. When 15,000 tiles are produced, total materials cost is £30,000.
>
> - The activity level has increased by 5,000 tiles which is 50% of the original level of 10,000 tiles.
>
> - The total materials cost has behaved in the same way: it has increased by £10,000 or 50% of the original level of £20,000.

- The materials cost per tile is £20,000/10,000 or £2 per tile when 10,000 are produced, and £30,000/15,000 or £2 per tile when 15,000 are produced: the materials cost per unit is the same however many units are produced.

- As the total cost varies directly in line with activity, with both changing by 50%, and the materials cost per unit remains the same whatever the level of activity, the materials cost of the tiles is said to be a variable cost.

Labour costs:

When 10,000 tiles are produced, total labour cost is £40,000. When 15,000 tiles are produced, total labour cost is £50,000.

- As before, the activity level has increased by 50%.

- The total labour cost has behaved differently: it has increased by £10,000, but this is only 25% of the original level of £40,000.

- The labour cost per tile is £40,000/10,000 or £4 per tile when 10,000 are produced, and £50,000/15,000 or £3.33 per tile when 15,000 are produced: the labour cost per unit changes with the number of units produced, so labour is not a variable cost. It cannot be a fixed cost.

- As the total labour does not vary directly in line with activity, the labour cost is said to be a semi-variable cost.

Expenses:

When 10,000 tiles are produced, expenses are £25,000. When 15,000 tiles are produced, expenses are still £25,000.

- As before, the activity level has increased by 50%.

- The expenses per tile are £25,000/10,000 or £2.50 per tile when 10,000 are produced, and £25,000/15,000 or £1.67 per tile when 15,000 are produced: the expenses cost per unit changes with the number of units produced.

- The expenses have not changed at all.

- As expenses do not vary at all in line with activity, expenses are said to be a fixed cost.

Note that in most manufacturing organisations, materials are usually variable costs, and labour is usually either a variable or a semi-variable cost of production. Expenses are usually semi-variable or fixed.

We will work through a further example now that gives you an idea of how the different types of cost behaviour affect the cost of a single unit of production.

Illustration 2 Materials, labour and expenses

Toys 4 U is a company that makes children's toys. One of its top selling lines is a 'Chunker', a chunky plastic car that can be assembled by a child. The plastic components are bought in at a cost of 90p per car. The company packages these in boxes which cost 20p each. The labour used for the packaging operation costs 20p per unit.

Each Chunker made has a variable cost of:	£
Materials (90p + 20p)	1.10
Labour	0.20
Variable cost	1.30

If Toys 4 U made no Chunkers at all, there would be no cost at all. If it made 10 Chunkers, it would cost £13. If it made 5,000 Chunkers, it would cost the company £6,500, and so on.

2 Graphs

2.1 Variable costs

If we plot a graph of the total variable cost on the y-axis and the level of output on the x-axis, we would have an upward-sloping straight line which passes through the origin (0,0).

2.1.1 Graph of total variable cost

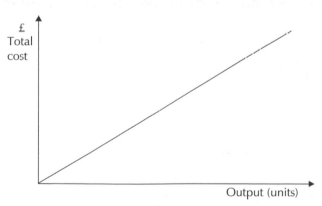

Materials and labour costs in the production department are usually mostly variable costs, although bulk discounts when purchasing materials and a fixed number of production employees may affect them. As a general rule, because the cost is spent directly on each unit of production, variable cost will be the same amount for each unit, so a graph of **unit cost** against level of output would be a horizontal line; no matter how many are produced, the unit cost will be the same for each unit.

2.1.2 Graph of variable cost per unit

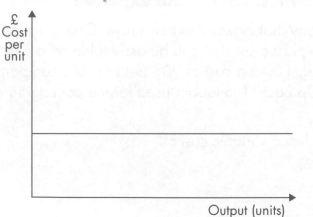

2.2 Fixed costs

Some materials and labour costs in the production department, and most expenses or overheads, are fixed costs which are not affected by changes in production level. They remain the same in total whether no units are produced or many units are produced. They are incurred in relation to a period of time rather than production level, and are sometimes referred to as **period costs**. Examples are:

- The salary of a supervisor
- The rent of a factory
- Straight-line depreciation of plant and machinery where the same amount is charged in each year

A graph of total fixed costs against output level produces a horizontal line.

2.2.1 Graph of total fixed costs

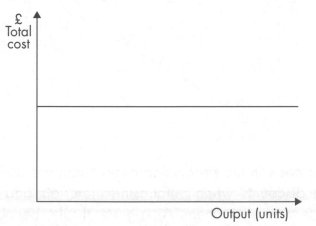

Because fixed costs remain the same at different output levels, if a fixed cost per unit is calculated, this will decrease as output increases as the same cost is spread over more units, so each unit attracts a smaller share. This gives management an incentive to increase production as it means that each unit is cheaper to produce. This is demonstrated in the following graph.

2.2.2 Graph of fixed cost per unit

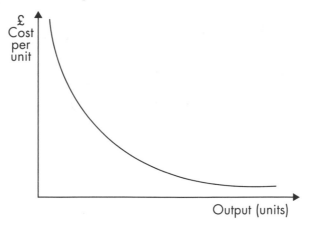

Activity 1: Fixed cost per unit

Sleet Ltd makes garden benches and incurs fixed costs of £20,000 per year.

Required

Calculate the fixed cost per garden bench at the following output levels, completing the entries in the table below.

Output level (units)	Fixed cost per bench £
1,000	
10,000	
20,000	
100,000	

2.3 Semi-variable costs

A semi-variable cost has both a fixed element and a variable element. One example of an overhead that is a semi-variable cost is electricity: the business faces a basic charge for the period plus a per unit consumption charge. Employees paid a basic wage plus bonus are also a semi-variable cost.

The graph for a semi-variable cost in total is upward sloping, like the variable cost graph, but starts part of the way up the y-axis at the level of the fixed cost element.

...ed or variable by putting a ...elow.

	Fixed	Variable
...g yard		

...point

...estion may give you a list of costs and ask you to identify whether ...e, fixed or semi-variable costs.

3: Fixed, variable or semi-variable cost

...o Ltd manufactures sports cars.

...quired

...lassify the following costs by their behaviour (fixed, variable or semi-variable) by putting a tick in the relevant column of the following table.

Cost	Fixed	Variable	Semi-variable
Employees in the factory paid on a piecework basis (per car produced)			
Hire of specialist tuning equipment, consisting of a monthly payment plus a usage charge			
Yearly payment for design costs			
Metal used in the manufacture of the cars			

Activity 4: Costs at different levels of production

Identify the type of cost behaviour (fixed, variable or semi-variable) described in each statement by placing a tick in the relevant column of the table.

Statement	Fixed	Variable	Semi-variable
At 6,000 units, this cost is £21,000, and at 8,750 units, it is £30,625			
At 4,000 units, this cost is £5.00 per unit, and at 5,000 units it is £4.00 per unit			
At 9,000 units this cost is £45,500, and at 11,000 units, this cost is £51,500			

Activity 5: Unit cost

Chelmport Ltd makes a single product. A production level of 50,000 units has the following costs:

Materials   20,000 kilos at £20 per kilo
Labour   10,000 hours at £15 per hour
Overheads   £500,000

Required

Complete the table below to show the unit product cost at the production of 50,000 units.

Element	Unit product cost £
Materials	
Labour	
Direct cost	
Overheads	
Total	

3 The high–low method

The **high–low method** can be used to estimate the fixed and variable parts of a semi-variable cost. It requires several observations of the costs incurred at different output levels, such as would be recorded over a number of accounting periods. This data can then be used to predict costs that would be incurred at other output levels.

Illustration 3 High–low method

Over the last five years, Stormbreak Ltd has recorded the following costs:

Year	Output Units	Total cost £
20X1	32,000	505,000
20X2	37,000	580,000
20X3	48,000	745,000
20X4	53,000	820,000
20X5	51,000	790,000

Stormbreak Ltd wants to estimate the cost for 20X6, when they expect to produce 52,000 units.

This problem can be tackled by following four steps.

Step 1

Identify the high and low output and associated costs.

Look carefully at the information given and identify the highest and lowest output levels. Write these down, along with the total costs at those levels. (Don't be put off by any other information, such as the year, or the order in which the data is given; even if the cost column is given first, it is the highest and lowest outputs that matter.)

	Output Units	Total cost £
Highest	53,000	820,000
Lowest	32,000	505,000

Step 2

Deduct the lowest output/costs from the highest output/costs.

	Output Units	Total cost £
Highest	53,000	820,000
Lowest	32,000	505,000
Increase	21,000	315,000

This tells us that an increase of 21,000 units has led to an increase in costs of £315,000. This is due to the variable costs only, and gives us the figures we need for the next step.

Step 3

Calculate the variable cost per unit.

$$\text{Variable cost per unit} = \frac{\text{High cost} - \text{Low cost}}{\text{High output} - \text{Low output}}$$
$$= \frac{£315,000}{21,000}$$
$$= £15$$

Step 4

Find the fixed costs at one of the output levels used in the above calculations.

Choose either the highest or the lowest output level. Both will give the same result. Calculate the variable cost by taking the cost per unit from Step 3 multiplied by the number of units of output. Deduct this from the total cost at the same level of output and you will be left with the fixed cost.

At 53,000 units:

	£
Total cost	820,000
Less variable cost (53,000 × £15)	795,000
= fixed cost	25,000

At 32,000 units (as a check):

	£
Total cost	505,000
Less variable cost (32,000 × £15)	480,000
= fixed cost	25,000

Now we are in a position to answer the actual question asked, which is 'What are the expected costs when output is 52,000 units?' All we need to do is build up the total cost from the fixed and variable elements at this level of output.

	£
Fixed cost	25,000
Add variable cost (52,000 × £15)	780,000
= total cost	805,000

Activity 6: High–low method 1

Sunny Ltd has recorded the following total costs over the past six months:

Month	Production volume Units	Total cost £
January	3,500	47,000
February	2,900	41,000
March	3,300	45,000
April	3,700	49,000
May	4,200	54,000
June	4,000	52,000

Required

Estimate Sunny Ltd's fixed costs using the high–low technique.

Fixed cost = £ [   ]

Activity 7: High–low method 2

Complete the table below by inserting all costs for an activity level of 7,500 units.

£	6,000 units	7,500 units	8,000 units
Variable cost			
Fixed cost			
Total cost	97,000		115,000

Assessment focus point

An assessment question may give you the total costs at two activity levels and ask you to calculate the fixed and variable elements.

Chapter summary

- Costs can be classified according to their behaviour: fixed, variable, semi-variable.

- The total amount of a variable cost changes directly in line with changes in activity levels. The variable cost per unit is constant, whatever the activity level.

- The total amount of a fixed cost does not change in line with activity levels within a certain range. The fixed cost per unit declines as activity levels rise within that range.

- The total amount of a semi-variable cost changes in line with a change in activity level but not at the same rate, because part of the cost is fixed.

- The high-low technique can be used to find the variable and fixed elements of a semi-variable cost by identifying the costs at the highest and lowest levels of output.

Keywords

- **Cost behaviour:** The way a cost changes as production quantity or activity level changes

- **Fixed costs:** Do not vary with changes in production level within a certain range. They are incurred in relation to a period rather than a product

- **High–low method:** A method for estimating the fixed and variable parts of a semi-variable cost

- **Period costs:** Costs which relate to a time period rather than the output of products or services

- **Semi-variable costs:** Costs which have both a fixed element and a variable element, so they vary as activity varies but not to the same degree

- **Variable costs:** Vary according to the level of production

- **Unit cost:** The cost of each individual unit produced by the business or service provided

1 **Complete the following sketch graphs with the correct labels on each axis, and plot the cost.**

   (a)   Total fixed cost

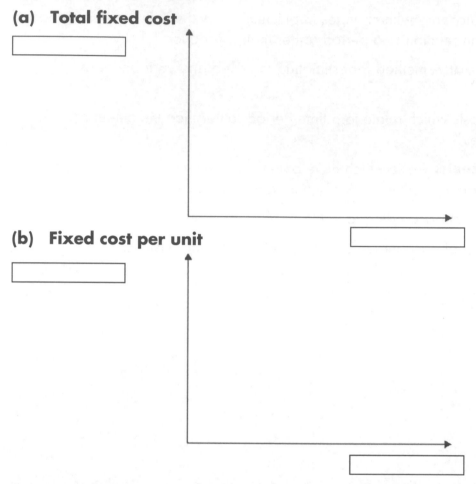

   (b)   Fixed cost per unit

2 **For a manufacturer of bags, classify the following costs by their behaviour (fixed, variable or semi-variable) by putting a tick in the relevant column of the table below.**

Cost	Fixed	Variable	Semi-variable
Entertainment budget for the year			
Telephone costs that include a fixed line rental charge plus call charges			
Leather used in the production process			
Labour costs paid as production overtime			

3 **Identify the following statements as either true or false by putting a tick in the relevant column of the table below.**

Statement	True	False
Total variable costs do not change directly with changes in activity but variable costs per unit do		
Fixed costs per unit decrease with increasing levels of output		

4 **Identify the type of cost behaviour (fixed, variable or semi-variable) described in each statement by putting a tick in the relevant column of the table below.**

Statement	Fixed	Variable	Semi-variable
Costs of £4 per unit at 30,000 units and £24 per unit at 5,000 units			
Costs of £50,000 are made up of a fixed charge of £20,000 and a further cost of £10 per unit at 3,000 units			
Costs are £60,000 at 12,000 units and £35,000 at 7,000 units			

5 **Complete the table below by inserting all costs for an activity level of 12,000 units.**

£	6,500 units	12,000 units	13,500 units
Variable cost			
Fixed cost			
Total cost	17,500		31,500

Inventory classification and valuation

5

Learning outcomes

1.2	**Recognise common costing techniques used in an organisation** • Inventory valuation methods: first-in-first-out (FIFO), last-in-last-out (LIFO), weighted average cost (AVCO)
1.6	**Identify how materials, labour and overheads are classified and recorded** • The components and construction of a manufacturing account
2.1	**Calculate cost of inventory issues and inventory valuation** • Cost issue of inventory for management accounting purposes using FIFO, LIFO and AVCO • Calculate closing values of inventory using FIFO, LIFO and AVCO (rounding figures as necessary)
2.5	**Calculate the direct cost of a product** • How direct cost is a component of product cost • Calculate direct cost of a product in a manufacturing organisation taking into account the flow of inventory in the production process, what constitutes direct cost, manufacturing cost, cost of goods manufactured and cost of goods sold

Assessment context

This is a topic that is expected to feature in the computer-based test.

Qualification context

This section introduces fundamental methods to value inventory that will also be seen in the *Management Accounting: Costing* unit at Level 3.

Business context

Businesses need to adopt an appropriate method of valuing inventory on a consistent basis to ensure profit is correctly stated in the financial accounts.

Chapter overview

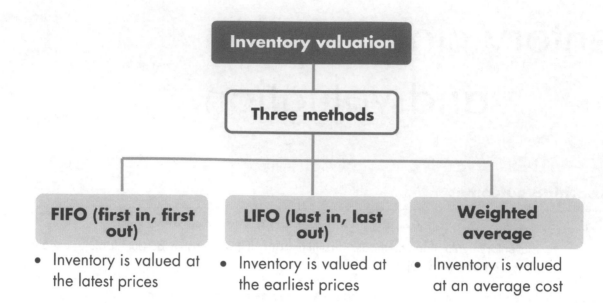

Inventory valuation

Three methods

FIFO (first in, first out)
- Inventory is valued at the latest prices

LIFO (last in, last out)
- Inventory is valued at the earliest prices

Weighted average
- Inventory is valued at an average cost

Introduction

We looked at materials in Chapter 2 when we considered how costs are classified. Now we look at the **inventory** (or stock) of materials and other items kept by the business, either for use in production or, ultimately, for resale.

Inventory is a collective term used to describe items held by the business, and which (for this unit) can be included in one of the following categories:

- **Raw materials** and components for incorporation into products, plus consumables

- **Finished goods** that have been completed ready for sale, plus bought-in **goods purchased for resale**

- Part-finished goods (**work-in-progress** or **WIP**), which are items of which manufacture has begun but has only been partly completed

1 Inventory records

Most businesses keep track of the quantities of raw materials that they have in inventory by maintaining an inventory record for each type of material held. This is updated each time material is received into, or issued from, stores, and a new balance of inventory held is calculated.

1.1 Inventory cards

Inventory cards are manual records that are written up and kept in the stores department. An example is shown here.

INVENTORY CARD

Description: Blue plastic-coated fabric (1.8m wide)

Code No: B6309582

Inventory: metres
units

Inventory No: 582
Maximum: 250
Minimum: 20
Reorder level: 40
Reorder quantity: 200

Receipts			Issues			Balance
Date	Reference	Quantity	Date	Reference	Quantity	Quantity
20X6			20X6			
1 May						40
11 May	GRN 0067	200				240
			12 May	MR 296	30	210
			14 May	MR 304	20	190
			15 May	MR 309	50	140
13 May	MRN 127	10				150

The information on the inventory card gives all the details the storekeeper needs to know such as:

- Issues to production: date, quantity and a reference to the **materials requisition** (MR), which is the document that the production department uses to request material from stores. The materials requisition is also sometimes called a purchase requisition.

- Receipts: date, quantity and details of the **goods received note (GRN)** for goods delivered to the business. A GRN is raised in the goods inwards department to confirm the quantity and type of goods received from suppliers.

- Balance: the quantity of inventory on hand after each inventory movement.

1.2 Stores ledger account

The **stores ledger accounts** held by the accounts department are very similar to inventory cards. They carry all the information that an inventory card does, and they are updated from the same sources: GRNs and MRs. But there are two important differences:

(1) Cost details are recorded in the stores ledger account, so that the unit cost and total cost of each issue and receipt is shown. The balance of inventory after each inventory movement is also valued. The value is recorded as these accounts form part of the cost accounting system.

(2) The stores ledger accounts are written up and kept in the costing part of the accounts department, or in a stores office separate from the stores, by a clerk experienced in cost bookkeeping.

1.3 Purchase requisition (also called materials requisition)

A department requiring goods will complete a purchase requisition form asking the purchasing department to carry out the necessary transaction. It must be countersigned (authorised) by the supervisor or departmental head who is responsible for the department's budget.

The requisition is sent to the purchasing department, who will select an appropriate supplier.

MATERIALS REQUISITION

Material required for: _Job 3965_   No: 296
(job)

Department: _Toy production_   Date: _12 May 2006_

Quantity	Description	Code No	Price per unit	£
30	Blue plastic-coated fabric (1.8m wide)	B6309582		

Authorised by: ....._J Daniels_........................

1.4 Purchase order

A purchase order form is completed by the purchasing department. An order form should be sent, even if the order is made by telephone, to confirm that the order is legitimate.

The purchasing department will also keep a copy.

Purchase Order/Confirmation   Fenchurch Garden Centre
                                         Pickle Lane
                                         Westbridge
                                         Kent

Our Order Ref: Date
To:

⌐(Address)   ⌐   Please deliver to the above address
                                       Ordered by:
                                       Passed and checked by:
                                       Total Order Value £

L   ⌐

Ref	Quantity	Description	Unit Cost	Total
Q	200	Flower pot	0.05	10.00
			Subtotal	10.00
			VAT (@20%)	2.00
			Total	12.00

1.5 Goods received note

A GRN is completed upon delivery of the goods. It is completed on the basis of a physical check, counting items received and seeing that they are not damaged.

ACCOUNTS COPY

GOODS RECEIVED NOTE
STORES COPY

DATE: __7 March 20X1__   TIME: __2.00 pm____   NO 5565

ORDER NO: _____

SUPPLIER'S ADVICE NOTE NO: _____   WAREHOUSE A

QUANTITY	CAT NO	DESCRIPTION
20	TP 400	Terracotta pots, medium

RECEIVED IN GOOD CONDITION: L. W.   (INITIALS)

1.6 Invoice

An invoice from the supplier will be received by accounts, detailing the amount required to be paid.

Invoice

Fenchurch Garden Centre
Pickle Lane
Westbridge
Kent

To: ⌐ Customer name
      Address

Invoice number:
Date/Tax point:
Order number:
Account number:

Quantity	Description	Stock code	Unit Cost £	Total £
20	Terracotta pots, medium	TP400	8.00	160.00
			Net total	160.00
			VAT	32.00
			Invoice total	192.00

2 Inventory valuation methods

When goods are issued to the production department from stores or a warehouse, a value will need to be recorded on the stores ledger accounts and on the costing details for the job or department that is going to bear that cost. The question is how do we value these issues if prices are changing regularly? How should the remaining inventories on hand be valued? This is not just a costing problem; it is also something that is needed for the preparation of the financial accounts.

Some items can be specifically priced from an invoice as they are individual items, but for most materials that are bought in quantity and added to an existing inventory, this is not possible, so one of the following methods can be used to estimate the cost.

2.1 First in, first out (FIFO)

First in, first out (**FIFO**) assumes that the first items bought are the first items issued. So:

- Items issued are costed at the earliest invoice prices related to the inventory held, working forwards through to the later prices; and

- Inventory on hand is valued at the latest prices, working back.

FIFO is most appropriate in businesses where the oldest items are actually issued first, which is the case with perishable goods such as food, but actually this is a very popular method in many types of business.

Note that in a time of rising prices generally, FIFO values inventory at the highest amounts. This leads to a high value of closing inventory at the end of an accounting period, which can make that period's profit look better.

Say, for example, ABC Ltd's inventory consisted of four deliveries of raw material in the last month:

		Units		
1 September	1,000	at	£2.00
8 September	500	at	£2.50
15 September	500	at	£3.00
22 September	1,000	at	£3.50

If on 23 September 1,500 units were issued to production, 1,000 of these units would be priced at £2 (the cost of the 1,000 oldest units in inventory), and 500 at £2.50 (the cost of the next oldest 500). 1,000 units of closing inventory would be valued at £3.50 (the cost of the 1,000 most recent units received), and 500 units at £3.00 (the cost of the next most recent 500).

Note that FIFO (and **LIFO** and **AVCO**) are just methods for **accounting** for inventory. They are not used for **physically issuing** inventory. For example, the inventory is not necessarily issued on a first in, first out basis, it is just valued on a first in, first out basis.

2.2 Last in, first out (LIFO)

Last in, first out (LIFO) is the opposite of FIFO: it assumes that the last items bought are the first items issued. So:

- Items issued are costed at the latest invoice prices, working backwards through to the earlier prices; and

- Inventory on hand is valued at the earliest prices related to the inventory held, working forward.

LIFO may be deemed to be appropriate if new deliveries are physically piled on top of existing inventories, and goods issued are picked from the top of the pile. However, from a financial accounting point of view, LIFO is not a permitted method of inventory valuation, so in practice it is rarely seen.

Note that in times of general price inflation, LIFO means a lower value of inventory at the end of a period than FIFO, so that period's profit tends to look worse.

In the example above it will be 1,000 units of issues which will be valued at £3.50, and the other 500 units issued will be valued at £3.00. 1,000 units of closing inventory will be valued at £2.00, and 500 at £2.50.

2.3 Average cost (AVCO)

With this method, a weighted average cost is calculated each time a new delivery is received. The weighting is provided by the number of units at each price brought into the calculation. The general formula is

$$\text{Average price per unit} = \frac{\text{Total value of existing inventory} + \text{Total value of units added to inventory}}{\text{Units of existing inventory} + \text{Units added to inventory}}$$

AVCO would be most appropriate if the inventories are mixed when they are stored, for example chemicals stored in a vat.

When prices are generally rising, AVCO distorts period profits less than FIFO or LIFO, since it uses an average of the prices at which the actual inventory was purchased.

Illustration 1 FIFO, LIFO and AVCO

Peregrine Pet Supplies sells doggy beds which it buys from a manufacturer. The following transactions were recorded in September 20X6:

Date	Transaction type	Quantity	Unit purchase price £
1 September	Opening balance	50	10
3 September	Receipt	100	12
6 September	Issue to sell	110	
9 September	Receipt	100	13
15 September	Issue to sell	80	
21 September	Receipt	100	14

What would be the:

(a) Cost of issues
(b) Value of closing inventory

in the month of September using FIFO, LIFO and AVCO methods of valuation?

FIFO

Each time there is an issue of inventory we must calculate the cost of those items based upon the FIFO assumption.

---

6 September issue   110 units

These will be costed as follows:

	£
50 @ £10 (the opening balance)	500
60 @ £12 (60 of the 100 items received on 3 September)	720
Total cost of issue	1,220

40 units are left in inventory at £12 each.

15 September issue   80 units

	£
40 @ £12 (the remainder of the 3 September receipt)	480
40 @ £13 (40 of the 100 items received on 9 September)	520
Total cost of issue	1,000

60 units are left in inventory at £13 each.

30 September closing inventory valuation

	£
60 @ £13 (the remainder of the 9 September receipt)	780
100 @ £14 (all received on 21 September and still held)	1,400
Total value of inventory	2,180

This can then all be recorded on the stores ledger account as follows:

Stores ledger account			
	Quantity (units)	Cost per unit	Value £
1 Sept Opening balance	50	£10	500
3 Sept Receipt	100	£12	1,200
Balance	150		1,700
6 Sept Issue	(110)	(50 @ £10) + (60 @ £12)	(1,220)
Balance	40		480
9 Sept Receipt	100	£13	1,300
Balance	140		1,780
15 Sept Issue	(80)	(40 @ £12) + (40 @ £13)	(1,000)
Balance	60		780
21 Sept Receipt	100	£14	1,400
Balance	160		2,180

(a) Cost of issues:

= £1,220 + £1,000

= £2,220

(b) Value of closing inventory. This is the value of the balance on hand at the bottom of the calculation = £2,180.

You may also use the following format to complete a stores ledger account:

| | Stores ledger account | | | | | | | |
| | Receipts | | | Issues | | | Balance | |
Date	Quantity (units)	Cost per unit £	Value £	Quantity (units)	Cost per unit £	Value £	Quantity (units)	Value £
Balance at 1 Sept							50	500
3 Sept	100	12.00	1,200				150	1,700
6 Sept				50	10.00	500	40	480
				60	12.00	720		
9 Sept	100	13.00	1,300				140	1,780
15 Sept				40	12.00	480	60	780
				40	13.00	520		
21 Sept	100	14.00	1,400				160	2,180

LIFO

Each time there is an issue of inventory we must calculate the cost of those items based upon the LIFO assumption.

6 September issue   110 units

	£
100 @ £12 (the items received on 3 September)	1,200
10 @ £10 (10 of the 50 units in the opening balance)	100
Total cost of issue	1,300

40 units are left in inventory at £10 each.

15 September issue   80 units

	£
Total cost of issue: 80 @ £13 (80 of the 100 items received on 9 September)	1,040

60 units are left in inventory: 20 from the 9 September purchase at £13 each, and 40 from the opening balance at £10 each.

30 September closing inventory valuation

	£
100 @ £14 (all received on 21 September and still held)	1,400
20 @ £13 (the remainder of the 9 September receipt)	260
40 @ £10 (the remainder of the opening balance)	400
Total value of inventory	2,060

Again this can be recorded in the stores ledger account as follows:

		Quantity (units)	Cost per unit	Value £
1 Sept	Opening balance	50	£10	500
3 Sept	Receipt	100	£12	1,200
Balance		150		1,700
6 Sept	Issue	(110)	(100 @ £12) + (10 @ £10)	(1,300)
Balance		40		400
9 Sept	Receipt	100	£13	1,300
Balance		140		1,700
15 Sept	Issue	(80)	80 @ £13	(1,040)
Balance		60		660
21 Sept	Receipt	100	£14	1,400
Balance		160		2,060

(a)   Cost of issues   = £1,300 + £1,040

= £2,340

(b) Value of closing inventory = £2,060

Note that this is **not** the same as valuing at the earliest prices, which would be (50 @ £10) + (100 @ £12) + (10 @ £13) = £1,830. This is because we have already used up some of those earlier prices in costing the earlier issues.

We can complete the entries in the LIFO stores ledger account as follows:

| | Receipts | | | Issues | | | Balance | |
Date	Quantity (units)	Cost per unit £	Value £	Quantity (units)	Cost per unit £	Value £	Quantity (units)	Value £
Stores ledger account								
Balance at 1 Sept							50	500
3 Sept	100	12.00	1,200				150	1,700
6 Sept				100	12.00	1,200	40	400
				10	10.00	100		
9 Sept	100	13.00	1,300				140	1,700
15 Sept				80	13.00	1,040	60	660
21 Sept	100	14.00	1,400				160	2,060

AVCO

Under the AVCO method a weighted average price must be calculated after each receipt into inventory following a purchase. This average price is then used to cost the next issue, or to value the closing inventory. Here is the stores ledger account:

	Quantity (units)	Cost per unit	Value £
1 Sept Opening balance	50	£10	500.00
3 Sept Receipt	100	£12	1,200.00
Balance	150	£1,700/150 = £11.33	1,700.00
6 Sept Issue	(110)	£11.33	(1,246.30)
Balance	40		453.70
9 Sept Receipt	100	£13	1,300.00
Balance	140	£1,753.70/140 = £12.53	1,753.70
15 Sept Issue	(80)	£12.53	(1,002.40)
Balance	60		751.30
21 Sept Receipt	100	£14	1,400.00
Balance	160		2,151.30

(a) Cost of issues   = £1,246.30 + £1,002.40

  = £2,248.70

(b) Value of closing inventory = £2,151.30

The alternative format for the AVCO stores ledger account is as follows (we have rounded to the nearest whole number for reasons of space):

		Receipts			Issues			Balance	
Date	Quantity (units)	Cost per unit £	Value £	Quantity (units)	Cost per unit £	Value £	Quantity (units)	Value £
Balance at 1 Sept							50	500
3 Sept	100	12.00	1,200				150	1,700
6 Sept				110	11.33	1,246	40	454
9 Sept	100	13.00	1,300				140	1,754
15 Sept				80	12.53	1,002	60	752
21 Sept	100	14.00	1,400				160	2,152

Stores ledger account

Activity 1: Closing inventory values

The inventory record card for fountain pens needs to be completed for the following transactions.

1 March

(Opening inventory) : 100 units bought at £2 each

2 March : bought 300 units at £2.10 each

5 March : sold 50 units for £5 per unit

17 March : bought 100 units at £2.30 each

20 March : sold 150 units for £5 per unit

Required

(a) **Calculate the value of closing inventory at the end of March using FIFO, LIFO and AVCO methods by completing the tables below. For the AVCO method, the average cost per unit should be calculated to 3 decimal places.**

FIFO method

| Date | Receipts | | | Issues | | | Balance | |
	Quantity	Cost per unit £	Total cost £	Quantity	Cost per unit £	Total cost £	Quantity	Total cost £
1 Mar								
2 Mar								
5 Mar								
17 Mar								
20 Mar								

LIFO method

| Date | Receipts | | | Issues | | | Balance | |
	Quantity	Cost per unit £	Total cost £	Quantity	Cost per unit £	Total cost £	Quantity	Total cost £
1 Mar								
2 Mar								
5 Mar								
17 Mar								
20 Mar								

AVCO method

Date	Receipts Quantity	Receipts Cost per unit £	Receipts Total cost £	Issues Quantity	Issues Cost per unit £	Issues Total cost £	Balance Quantity	Balance Total cost £	Balance Avg. cost £
1 Mar									
2 Mar									
5 Mar									
17 Mar									
20 Mar									

(b) **Calculate the gross profit for March using FIFO, LIFO and AVCO methods.**

FIFO		LIFO		AVCO	
Sales revenue		Sales revenue		Sales revenue	
Less cost of sales		Less cost of sales		Less cost of sales	
Issues					
Gross profit		Gross profit		Gross profit	

Activity 2: Identifying inventory valuation methods 1

Required

Identify the correct inventory valuation method from the characteristic given by putting a tick in the relevant column in the table below.

	FIFO	LIFO	AVCO
Costs issues of inventory at the most recent purchase price			
Costs issues of inventory at the oldest purchase price			
Values closing inventory at the most recent purchase price			
Closing inventory is valued at the average of the cost of purchases			

Activity 3: Identifying inventory valuation methods 2

You are told the opening inventory of a single raw material in the stores is 1,000 units at £5.00 per unit. During the month 2,000 units at £6.00 per unit are received and the following week 1,800 units are issued.

Required

Identify the valuation method described in the statements below by putting a tick in the relevant column.

Statement	FIFO	LIFO	AVCO
The closing inventory is valued at £7,200			
The issue of 1,800 units is costed at £10,800			
The issue of 1,800 units is costed at £10,200			

You are told the opening inventory of a single raw material in the stores is 1,000 units at £5.00 per unit. During the month 2,000 units at £6.00 per unit are received and the following week 1,800 units are issued.

Required

Identify whether the statements in the table below are true or false by putting a tick in the relevant column.

Statement	True	False
AVCO values the closing inventory at £6,800		
FIFO costs the issue of 1,800 units at £12,800		
LIFO values the closing inventory at £6,200		

Activity 5: Cost of issues and inventory valuation

A business has the following movements of a certain type of inventory into and out of its stores for the month of March. There was no opening inventory.

Date	Receipts		Issues	
	Units	Cost £	Units	Cost £
1 March	700	3,500		
10 March	600	3,600		
15 March	200	1,600		
20 March			800	
25 March	300	2,700		

Required

Complete the table below by entering the cost of issues and closing inventory values. (Calculations performed to two decimal places.)

Method	Cost of issue on March 20 £	Closing inventory at March 31 £
FIFO		
LIFO		
AVCO		

3 Manufacturing account

Many manufacturing businesses are quite complex and have a variety of inventory lines, including materials, WIP and finished goods. For both financial and management accounting purposes they need to identify a figure for the cost of goods they have actually sold rather than retained as inventory in a period, and to do this they prepare a **manufacturing account** (also known as a cost statement for manufactured goods). The manufacturing account is prepared on the basis that only the costs of manufacturing the actual goods sold are included. To do this we must:

- Add in the cost of inventory held at the beginning of the period (of raw materials, part-finished goods and finished goods)

- Add in **direct costs** of raw materials purchased and labour, plus indirect costs and manufacturing expenses/overheads incurred in the period

- Deduct the cost of inventory (of all types) held at the end of the period, since these are carried forward and used up in the next period

The manufacturing account classifies inventory of raw materials, WIP and finished goods in arriving at:

- Prime cost
- Factory cost of goods produced
- Cost of goods sold

Illustration 2 Manufacturing account

Lama Ltd manufactures a range of products from a large number of raw materials. It is building up a picture of the costs it has incurred in making the products which it actually sold during 20X2.

First Lama Ltd wants to establish the cost of the direct materials used; that is, the cost of materials actually used in making items during the period (whether they are sold in the period or not). This is the cost of materials held at the beginning of the period plus new purchases, less what is left over at the end of the period (which will be used up in the next period):

	£
Opening inventory of raw materials	6,000
Purchases of raw materials	70,000
Less closing inventory of raw materials	(8,000)
DIRECT MATERIALS USED	68,000

Next Lama Ltd wants to identify the total direct cost of the items made. Sometimes known as prime cost, direct cost is the total cost of the direct materials used, plus the cost of direct labour:

	£
Direct materials used	68,000
Direct labour	37,900
DIRECT COST	105,900

To establish how much its manufacturing operation has cost in making items in the period; that is, its total manufacturing cost, Lama Ltd must next add in the manufacturing overheads incurred in the period. These comprise the indirect cost of materials, labour and expenses in the production department, such as grease and oil for the machines, supervisor salary, factory rent, machine depreciation, and factory light and heat. Collectively these are called manufacturing overheads.

	£
Direct cost	105,900
Manufacturing overheads	35,000
MANUFACTURING COST	140,900

However, this is not quite the full story. At least some of the materials, labour and overheads in the period were spent on finishing off items that were only part-complete at the start of the period, so the cost of opening WIP should be included (note that at this stage in your studies you do not have to arrive at a cost for WIP). Some costs were spent on part-completing items that were unfinished at the end of the period, so the cost of closing WIP should be deducted. The change in the level of WIP must therefore be taken into account to arrive at the cost of goods manufactured in the period:

	£
Manufacturing cost	140,900
Opening inventory of WIP	4,000
Less closing inventory of WIP	(4,900)
COST OF GOODS MANUFACTURED	140,000

To arrive at the final cost of goods sold, Lama Ltd must take account of the fact that, while the cost of opening finished goods inventory should be included in the cost, the value of closing inventory of finished goods should be excluded since they have not been sold:

	£
Cost of goods manufactured	140,000
Opening inventory of finished goods	56,000
Less closing inventory of finished goods	(47,000)
COST OF GOODS SOLD	149,000

Lama Ltd's cost of goods sold is therefore opening inventory (of all items) plus direct materials purchases, direct labour and manufacturing overheads less closing inventory of all items.

The full manufacturing account is as follows:

Lama Ltd: Manufacturing account for the year ended 31 March 20X2

	£
Opening inventory of raw materials	6,000
Purchases of raw materials	70,000
Closing inventory of raw materials	(8,000)
DIRECT MATERIALS USED	68,000
Direct labour	37,900
DIRECT COST	105,900
Manufacturing overheads	35,000
MANUFACTURING COST	140,900
Opening inventory of WIP	4,000
Closing inventory of WIP	(4,900)
COST OF GOODS MANUFACTURED	140,000
Opening inventory of finished goods	56,000
Closing inventory of finished goods	(47,000)
COST OF GOODS SOLD	149,000

Assessment focus point

You need to learn the order of the items in the account for your assessment.

You could be asked to determine the following costs in your assessment:

Direct material used

Direct cost

Manufacturing cost

Cost of goods manufactured

Cost of goods sold

Activity 6: Manufacturing account

A company has the following cost data for the month:

	£
Opening raw materials inventory	12,500
Raw materials purchases	47,000
Closing raw materials inventory	8,200
Opening WIP inventory	4,700
Closing WIP inventory	2,800
Opening finished goods inventory	27,600
Closing finished goods inventory	29,200
Direct labour costs	64,400
Manufacturing overhead costs	14,500

Required

Determine and enter the cost totals below.

Direct material used   £ ☐   Cost of goods manufactured   £ ☐

Direct cost   £ ☐   Cost of goods sold   £ ☐

Manufacturing cost   £ ☐

4 Calculating unit product cost

Having prepared the information that goes into the manufacturing account, we need to understand what it actually tells us.

A manufacturing account that covers a whole organisation, like Lama Ltd's, covers all product lines and all raw materials, labour and overheads, so it tells us how much it cost the organisation to produce all the goods which it actually sold in the period in question. This means it can calculate its **gross profit** overall, a financial accounting figure that appears in the published statement of profit or loss:

	£
Revenue	X
Cost of goods sold	(X)
Gross profit	X

4.1 Calculating unit product cost from the manufacturing account

If the organisation only has one product, or if the manufacturing account only relates to one product, we can use it to calculate a product cost per unit of output, or **unit product cost**. This is also sometimes known as a unit cost.

Illustration 3 Unit cost

Pringle Ltd makes and sells only one product in a simple process that means there is no WIP. It has prepared the following manufacturing account, for a period when it made 100,000 items and sold 120,000 items:

	£
Opening inventory of raw materials	5,000
Purchases of raw materials	49,000
Closing inventory of raw materials	(9,000)
DIRECT MATERIALS USED	45,000
Direct labour	105,000
DIRECT COST	150,000
Manufacturing overheads	55,000
MANUFACTURING COST (100,000 items)	205,000
Opening inventory of finished goods (30,000 items)	56,000
Closing inventory of finished goods (10,000 items)	(21,000)
COST OF GOODS SOLD (120,000 items)	240,000

There are three useful figures that we can calculate from this information:

- The direct cost (direct materials plus direct labour) of each of the 100,000 items manufactured in the period is £150,000/100,000 = £1.50 each.

- If manufacturing overheads are added in, the unit product cost of each of the 100,000 items manufactured is £205,000/100,000 = £2.05 each.

- The cost of each item actually sold in the period is £240,000/120,000 = £2.00 each.

You may be wondering why the unit product cost and the cost of each item actually sold are different amounts. This arises because the items sold include opening inventory (which we can see cost £56,000/30,000 = £1.87 each) as well as items produced in the period at £2.05 each. The effect of this is to bring the average cost per unit sold down to only £2.00 each.

4.2 Calculating unit product cost from cost information

A simpler way of calculating the direct cost per unit and the full unit product cost is possible when information on the materials, labour and expenses (or overheads) for a particular product is available:

- Materials: information on the total quantity of materials in kilograms, say, and their price per kilogram may be available for a certain level of production. The product unit cost of materials is:

$$\frac{\text{Total materials cost (kilograms} \times \text{price)}}{\text{Number of units}}$$

- Labour: information on the total number of direct hours and the time rate at which they are paid may be available for a certain level of production. The product unit cost of labour is:

$$\frac{\text{Total labour cost (hours} \times \text{time} - \text{rate)}}{\text{Number of units}}$$

- Expenses (or overheads): information on the total expenses may be available for a certain level of production.

Illustration 4 Unit cost from cost information

You are told that Lama Ltd made 140,000 items in the following year, 20X3.

- 280,000 kilograms of material were used at £0.30 per kilogram
- 14,700 hours of direct labour was used at £10 per hour
- Expenses were £70,000.

Lama Ltd's unit product cost in 20X3 is calculated as follows:

Element	Workings	Unit product cost £
Materials	(280,000 × £0.30)/140,000	0.60
Labour	(14,700 × £10)/140,000	1.05
Direct cost		1.65
Expenses	£70,000/140,000	0.50
Total		2.15

Chapter summary

- Inventory can be made up of raw materials for use in production, part-finished goods (work-in-progress or WIP) and finished goods.

- The quantity of each line of inventory will often be recorded on an inventory card – a stores ledger account is similar but this also includes the value of the inventory held.

- When materials are required from stores by a production department, or another department, the user department will issue a materials requisition detailing the goods required.

- The valuation of inventory normally requires an assumption to be made regarding the valuation method – this will be FIFO, LIFO or AVCO.

- A complete manufacturing account identifies the cost of goods sold in a period. It also identifies: the cost of direct materials used in manufacture; the direct cost of manufacturing; the total manufacturing cost; the cost of goods manufactured; and the cost of goods sold.

- The manufacturing account can be used to calculate product cost per unit manufactured.

- The unit product cost can also be calculated if information on the materials, labour and expenses (or overheads) for a particular product is available.

Keywords

- **AVCO:** A weighted average cost is calculated each time there is a receipt of inventory. Subsequent issues are costed and inventory on hand is valued at the most up to date weighted average cost

- **Cost of goods manufactured:** Manufacturing cost plus net inventory of WIP

- **Cost of goods sold:** Opening inventory of all items, plus purchases, direct labour and manufacturing overheads, less closing inventory of all items

- **Direct cost:** The total cost of direct materials used and direct labour

- **Direct materials used:** The cost of materials purchased in the period, plus the cost of opening inventory less the cost of closing inventory of materials

- **FIFO (first in, first out):** Assumes that items purchased earliest are issued first. Inventory on hand is valued at the latest prices, issues are costed at the earliest relevant prices

- **Goods received note (GRN):** A document raised in the goods inwards department to confirm the quantity, condition and type of goods received by them for the business's own records

- **Inventory:** Goods held by the business made up of raw materials including consumables, part-finished goods (WIP) and finished goods

- **LIFO (last in, first out):** Assumes that items purchased latest are issued first. Inventory on hand is valued at the earliest relevant prices and issues are costed at the latest prices

- **Manufacturing account:** A statement that analyses costs to show the cost of goods sold by a business

- **Manufacturing cost:** Direct cost plus manufacturing overheads

- **Materials requisition:** A request for materials by the production department sent to stores

- **Unit product cost:** The cost of each item manufactured if the full costs of direct materials, direct labour and expenses (manufacturing overheads) are included

Test your learning

1 **Classify the following items as raw materials, WIP or finished goods. (Tick the appropriate box.)**

	Raw materials	WIP	Finished goods
Bricks at a brick-making factory			
Bricks in stores at a building company			
The ingredients for making bricks held in stores at a brick-making company			
A brick that has been moulded but not fired in the kiln at a brick-making company			

2 **Using the following methods:**

(a) FIFO

(b) LIFO

(c) AVCO

Calculate the cost of materials issues and the value of closing inventory using the information below, and enter these into the stores ledger account. Show your workings underneath the account.

3 Jan	Balance	100 kg	Valued @ £8.80 per kg
16 Jan	Received	400 kg	£9 per kg
27 Jan	Issued	250 kg	
5 Feb	Issued	180 kg	
9 Feb	Received	400 kg	£9.30 per kg
17 Feb	Issued	420 kg	
25 Feb	Received	500 kg	£9.35 per kg

FIFO

| Date | Receipts | | | Issues | | | Balance | |
	Quantity (kg)	Cost per kg £	Value £	Quantity (kg)	Cost per kg £	Value £	Quantity (kg)	Value £

Stores Ledger Account

LIFO

	Stores Ledger Account							
	Receipts			Issues			Balance	
Date	Quantity (kg)	Cost per kg £	Value £	Quantity (kg)	Cost per kg £	Value £	Quantity (kg)	Value £

AVCO

	Stores Ledger Account							
	Receipts			Issues			Balance	
Date	Quantity (kg)	Cost per kg £	Value £	Quantity (kg)	Cost per kg £	Value £	Quantity (kg)	Value £

3 **Identify whether the following statements are true or false by putting a tick in the relevant column of the table below.**

Statement	True	False
FIFO costs issues of inventory at the oldest purchase price		
AVCO costs issues of inventory at the most recent purchase price		
LIFO costs issues of inventory at the most recent purchase price		
FIFO values closing inventory at the oldest purchase price		
LIFO values closing inventory at the oldest purchase price		
AVCO values closing inventory at an average purchase price		

4 A business has the following movements in a certain type of inventory into and out of its stores for the month of October:

Date	Receipts	Total cost	Issues
	Units	£	Units
3 Oct	200	360	
7 Oct	160	360	
11 Oct			90
19 Oct	100	240	
24 Oct	70	160	

Required

Complete the table below for the cost of the issue on 11 October and the value of closing inventory on 31 October.

Method	Cost of issue on 11 Oct	Closing inventory at 31 Oct
	£	£
FIFO		
LIFO		
AVCO		

Labour costs and overheads

Learning outcomes

1.2	Recognise common costing techniques used in an organisation
	• Labour costing methods: time rate, overtime, piecework, bonus payments
	• Overhead absorption methods: per unit, labour hours, machine hours
2.2	Calculate labour payments
	• Calculate labour payments: time rate and overtime, piecework, bonuses
2.3	Calculate overhead absorption rates
	• Calculate simple overhead absorption rates: per unit, labour hours, machine hours (rounding figures as necessary) to show differing methods to arrive at unit cost

Assessment context

As with material costs seen in an earlier section, the labour cost and overhead cost within a manufacturing or service organisation is a key area. Expect to see questions on these topics in the computer-based test.

Qualification context

This chapter classifies labour costs into direct and indirect costs for costing purposes. It also deals with overheads.

Business context

Labour is a major cost for all businesses, although in the modern business environment this cost has reduced for manufacturing organisations relying on technology. Overheads have increased in the modern business environment.

Chapter overview

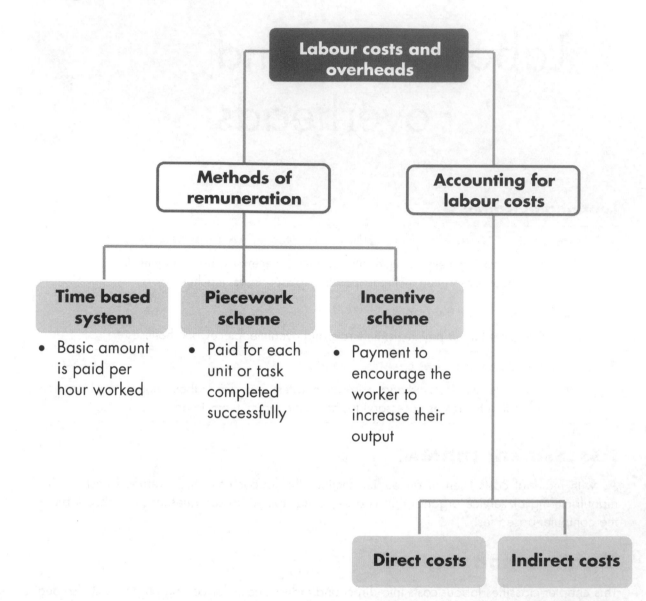

Introduction

This chapter looks at two of the major costs that a business incurs, labour and overheads. For management accounting purposes it is often necessary to analyse the gross pay of employees in detail. We mainly talk about the gross wage of the employee, but don't forget that there are other costs which can be considered to be labour costs, such as employer's national insurance, employer's pension contributions, training costs, and benefits such as company cars. All employees give rise to labour costs, the nature of which varies depending on what they do.

Labour costs associated with office workers in administration departments, canteen staff, maintenance staff and supervisory staff are **indirect costs**.

Costs arising from the employees who work directly on the goods produced by a manufacturing business, or employees who provide the service in a service business, are mostly **direct costs**.

1 Remuneration methods

1.1 Time rate

A **time rate** means that a basic amount is paid per hour worked.

> Wages = Hours worked × Basic rate of pay per hour

If the hours worked exceed a pre-set maximum, overtime is paid at a higher **overtime time rate**. In the assessment you may well be asked to calculate the gross wage for labour, separating out the cost of hours at the basic time rate (basic wage) from the cost of hours at the overtime time rate (overtime).

Illustration 1 Time rate and overtime

Finch Ltd has an overtime rate of time and a third for all complete hours worked over 35 hours per week. Peter is paid a basic wage of £9 per hour. During the week ending 24 March he worked a total of 39 hours. Work out Peter's gross wage for the week.

	£
Basic hours at time rate (35 × £9)	315
Overtime hours at overtime time rate (4 × £9 × $1\frac{1}{3}$)	48
Gross wage for the week	363

Some businesses treat basic wage for all hours worked as a direct cost, but the amount paid extra for overtime (called the 'overtime premium') as an indirect cost for costing purposes. This way, all units produced are costed at the basic labour cost, irrespective of whether they were produced during normal working hours or at the weekend, for example, when overtime was being paid.

Illustration 2 Overtime premium

Peter's total overtime in the case of Finch Ltd is £48. This comprises two elements:

(a) The basic element is the basic wage at the basic time rate × additional hours worked, in this case 4 hours × £9 = £36.

(b) The overtime premium is the extra paid on top of the basic rate for the additional hours worked. In this case the hourly premium is £9 × 1/3 = £3. The total overtime premium is therefore 4 hours × £3 = £12. It is this amount that some businesses may treat as an indirect cost, with the remainder of gross wage – £351 – treated as direct cost.

Note, however, that if the overtime is worked at the request of a customer so that an order can be completed within a certain time, the overtime premium is a direct cost of that particular order.

Assessment focus point

An assessment question may ask you to calculate a basic wage, overtime and gross wage for an employee.

Activity 1: Normal time and overtime 1

Mr Trent is a contract worker for Lyme Ltd. He charges the company £4 per hour for his services. He is paid overtime at time and a half. He works a standard 35 hour week.

Last week Mr Trent worked 40 hours.

Required

How much should he invoice Lyme Ltd for the work he has performed? Write your answers in the spaces provided below.

	Hours	Rate per hour	£
Normal time			
Overtime			
Total			

Activity 2: Normal time and overtime 2

Duesouth Ltd pays a time rate of £8.00 per hour for a 40 hour week.

Any employee working in excess of 40 hours per week is paid an overtime rate of £12.00 per hour.

Required

Calculate the basic wage, overtime and gross wage for the week for the two employees in the table below.

Employee	Hours worked	Basic wage £	Overtime £	Gross wage £
Y. Sterling	42			
T. Bindon	46			

1.2 Deductions

Deductions are made from employees' gross pay.
Compulsory deductions:

- Income tax (PAYE)
- Employees' National Insurance

Voluntary deductions:

- Pension contributions
- SAYE (save as you earn)
- Subscriptions

In addition to the gross pay employers pay Employer's National Insurance. Employer's National Insurance Contributions (NIC) will sometimes be part of labour cost, but some organisations show it as an expense.

Activity 3: Net pay calculation

Mr River also works for Lyme Ltd.

He is paid £6 per hour and works a standard 40 hour week. He is paid overtime at time and a half.

Each week PAYE of 25% and Employees' National Insurance of 10% is deducted from Mr River's pay before he is paid.

In the week ended 31 March 20X1, Mr Rivers worked a 42 hour week.

Required

What is Mr River's net pay that he receives in cash for the week ended 31 March 20X1? Insert your answers in the table below.

	Hours	Rate per hour	£
Basic pay			
Overtime premium			
Gross pay			
PAYE			
Employees' NIC			
NET PAY			

1.3 Piecework

With **piecework**, an amount is paid for each unit or task successfully completed, acting as an **incentive** to produce more. This method of remuneration can only be used in certain situations, that is, when there are specific, measurable tasks to be done which are not affected by other employees' performances.

Differential piecework offers higher rates as production increases. For example, 5p per unit may be paid for production of up to 2,000 units per week, rising to 7p per unit for 2,001 to 3,000 units, and so on.

Activity 4: Piecework pay 1

A company pays its employees using a differential piecework scheme. The rates are as follows:

Units per week	Cost per unit
0–100	£4
101–150	£4.50
151–200	£5
201+	£5.50

Required

If an employee produces 163 units in week 48, what would their gross pay be for that week? Write your answer below.

£	

Activity 5: Piecework pay 2

Identify the following statements about the piecework method as either true or false by putting a tick in the relevant column of the table below.

Statement	True	False
Employees' pay will remain the same if more units are produced		
An employee is paid 40p per unit and earns £340 for a production of 850 units		
An employee who is paid £420 for a production of 700 units is paid 60p per unit		
Employees' pay will decrease if less units are produced		

1.4 Bonus systems

A **bonus system** involves paying a bonus if output is better than expected. This will be in addition to the basic wage at the normal time rate and overtime at the overtime rate. The trigger for the payment of a bonus depends on the type of system that operates.

- A time-saved bonus is paid if the employee performs a task in a shorter time than the standard time allowed.

- A discretionary bonus is paid if the employer judges that the employee deserves one.

- A group bonus scheme pays a bonus to all workers who contributed to a successful job.

- A profit-sharing scheme pays a proportion of the business's profits to employees, the proportion paid often reflecting the level of responsibility.

Illustration 3 Bonuses

Sam, Jamil and Luka are paid £10.00 an hour and are expected to make 20 units an hour. For any excess production they are paid a bonus of 30p per unit.

Sam works a 35-hour week and produces 730 units.

Jamil works 40 hours and makes 790 units.

Luka works 32 hours and makes 700 units.

What is each employee's gross wage for the week?

Sam's expected output is $35 \times 20 = 700$ units. Producing 730 units means there is a bonus in respect of 30 items, so Sam's gross wage is $(35 \times £10) + (30 \times £0.30) = £359$.

Jamil's expected output is $40 \times 20 = 800$ units. Producing 790 units means there is no bonus, though the scheme does not mean that Jamil loses any pay for achieving less than the target production. Jamil's gross wage is simply $40 \times £10 = £400$.

Luka's expected output is $32 \times 20 = 640$ units. Producing 700 units means there is a bonus in respect of 60 items, so Luka's gross wage is $(32 \times £10) + (60 \times £0.30) = £338$.

Assessment focus point

An assessment question may ask you to calculate time rate wages, piecework wages and bonuses.

Activity 6: Time based pay plus bonus and piecework pay

Pyllon Ltd wishes to pay its employees using either the time-rate method with bonus or the piecework method.

The time-rate used is £10 per hour and an employee is expected to produce 15 units per hour; anything over this and the employee is paid a bonus of £0.50 per unit.

The piecework payment rate is £1.00 per unit.

Required

Complete the table below for the two methods showing the gross wage for the time-rate with bonus and the piecework wage.

Note. **If no bonus is paid, you should enter 0 as the bonus for that employee in the table.**

Hours worked	Unit output	Basic wage £	Bonus £	Gross wage £	Piecework wage £
30	400				
40	660				

Activity 7: Time based pay plus bonus

An employee is paid £10.00 an hour and is expected to make 20 units an hour.

Any excess production will be paid a bonus of 50p per unit.

Required

Identify the following statements as being true or false by putting a tick in the relevant column of the table below.

Statement	True	False
During a 40-hour week an employee produces 820 units and does not receive a bonus		
During a 36-hour week an employee produces 750 units and receives a bonus of £15		
During a 42-hour week an employee produces 900 units and receives total pay of £450		

1.5 Salary

Employees on a monthly salary are paid one-twelfth of their agreed annual salary each month. Overtime, bonuses and commissions on sales, for example, can be paid on top of this. Salaries in manufacturing businesses tend to relate to indirect costs such as office staff and factory supervisors. In some service sector businesses, however, salaried staff are a direct cost of providing the service, such as solicitors and accountants.

2 Recording labour costs

Information on labour hours worked and rates of pay is needed by two departments:

- The payroll department needs to know so that the amount that each employee has earned can be worked out.

- The management accounting department needs to know so that the labour cost of each task or unit of product can be calculated.

2.1 Direct and indirect costs

As we mentioned above, labour can be a direct or indirect cost. The table below shows in more detail how the costs will break down.

	Direct workers	Indirect workers
Normal Basic Pay	Direct cost	Indirect cost
General production: Overtime – Basic pay element	Direct cost	Indirect cost
General production: Overtime – O/T premium	Indirect cost	Indirect cost
General non-production: Overtime – Basic pay element	Indirect cost	Indirect cost
General non-production: Overtime – O/T premium	Indirect cost	Indirect cost
Specific overtime: Basic pay element	Direct cost	Direct cost
Specific overtime: O/T premium	Direct cost	Direct cost

Activity 8: Direct and indirect labour costs

Company X employs two types of labour: skilled workers, considered to be direct workers, and semi-skilled workers, considered to be indirect workers. Skilled workers are paid £10 per hour and semi-skilled £7.50 per hour. All employees work a standard 35 hour week. There are 7 skilled workers and 4 semi-skilled workers.

The skilled workers have worked 50 hours of overtime this week, 20 hours on a specific order and 30 hours on general production.

The semi-skilled workers have worked 20 hours of overtime, 10 hours on a specific order at a customer's request and the remaining 10 hours to meet general production requirements.

All overtime is paid at time and a half.

Required

Complete the table below which computes the total direct and indirect labour costs for the week. If a figure is 0 or a cell is blank, insert 0.

	Hours	Rate/hour	Direct cost £	Indirect cost £
Skilled workers				
Basic pay (normal hours)				
Basic pay (general overtime)				
Specific overtime				
Overtime premium (general overtime)				
Semi-skilled workers				
Basic pay (normal hours)				
Specific overtime				
General overtime				

2.2 Job costing

Many businesses perform work on particular jobs or tasks, often for particular clients, such as a construction company building an office block, a manufacturer of complex or unique items such as train rolling stock, or an accountancy firm conducting an audit. In such cases it is important to collect together all the costs, including labour costs, that relate to each particular job, not least because this will affect how much the client is charged. This is called job costing. This will be considered in more detail in your Level 3 studies, but it is useful to have a basic understanding.

3 Overheads

Businesses need to cost their production throughout the year, not just at the end of an accounting period. Therefore they predetermine or estimate their overheads for the year in advance and decide how to charge a proportion of the overheads to each cost unit. **Overhead absorption rates** are set for the year in advance, based on the budgeted overheads and the budgeted level of activity.

Formula to learn

OAR (overhead absorption rate) = $\dfrac{\text{Total budgeted production overhead}}{\text{Total budgeted activity level}}$

Formula to learn

Amount absorbed into production = Actual production activity × OAR

This occurs during the year or month as production takes place.

Illustration 4 Overhead absorption rates

Bluebell Electronics makes two products, the Videobooster and the Blastbox. It is trying to decide on an appropriate basis for the absorption of overheads. The following budgeted information is provided.

Production units	Videobooster 4,000		Blastbox 6,000	
	Components shop hours	Assembly hours	Components shop hours	Assembly hours
Direct labour:				
Hours per unit	1.25	0.5	2	1
Total hours	5,000	2,000	12,000	6,000
Machine hours:				
Per unit	2	1	0.3	0.2
Total hours	8,000	4,000	1,800	1,200

Calculate:

(a) Separate departmental overhead absorption rates using first labour hours and then machine hours as the absorption basis

(b) The overhead absorbed by each product under each of the overhead absorption bases

Note. The overheads for the two production cost centres were: Components shop, £32,375; and Assembly, £19,575.

(a) Departmental absorption rates

		Components	Assembly
Rate per direct labour hour			
$\dfrac{\text{Overheads}}{\text{Direct labour hours}}$	=	$\dfrac{£32,375}{5,000+12,000}$	$\dfrac{£19,575}{2,000+6,000}$
	=	£1.90 per direct labour hour	£2.45 per direct labour hour
Rate per machine hour			
$\dfrac{\text{Overheads}}{\text{Machine hours}}$	=	$\dfrac{£32,375}{8,000+1,800}$	$\dfrac{£19,575}{4,000+1,200}$
	=	£3.30 per machine hour	£3.76 per machine hour

(b) The overhead absorbed by each product

Rate per direct labour hour

	Videobooster	£	Blastbox	£
Components shop	£1.90 × 1.25h	2.38	£1.90 × 2h	3.80
Assembly	£2.45 × 0.5h	1.23	£2.45 × 1h	2.45
Total absorbed per unit		3.61		6.25

Rate per machine hour

	Videobooster	£	Blastbox	£
Components shop	£3.30 × 2h	6.60	£3.30 × 0.3	0.99
Assembly	£3.76 × 1h	3.76	£3.76 × 0.2	0.75
Total absorbed per unit		10.36		1.74

Assessment focus point

An assessment question may ask you to calculate overhead absorption rates based on machine hours, labour hours or units.

Activity 9: Overhead absorption rate

Alex Ltd is looking to calculate the unit cost for one of the products it makes. It needs to calculate an overhead absorption rate to apply to each unit.

The methods it is considering are:

- Per machine hour
- Per labour hour
- Per unit

Total factory activity for all production is forecast as follows:

Machine hours: 35,000
Labour hours: 20,000
Units: 58,000
Overheads: £500,000

Required

Complete the table below to show the possible overhead absorption rates that Alex Ltd could use. The absorption rates should be calculated to two decimal places.

	Machine hour	Labour hour	Unit
Overheads (£)			
Activity			
Absorption rate (£)			

Chapter summary

- Remuneration methods generally fall into one of the following categories:

  - Time rate and overtime time rate
  - Piecework
  - Bonus system
  - Salary

- Units of product are given a proportion of the overhead cost using an overhead absorption rate.

- The absorption rate is calculated by dividing the budgeted overhead by the budgeted level of activity.

Keywords

- **Bonus system:** The payment of an amount in addition to the time rate if a target is exceeded

- **Differential piecework:** The piecework rate increases for additional units over and above a pre-set quantity

- **Incentive:** In piecework systems, the incentive of being paid to complete each extra unit or task encourages the worker to increase their output

- **Overhead absorption rate:** Budgeted overhead divided by budgeted activity level

- **Overtime premium:** The additional cost of overtime hours above the basic time rate for those hours

- **Overtime time rate:** A higher rate of pay is paid if hours worked in a week exceed a pre-set limit

- **Piecework:** An amount is paid for each unit or task successfully completed

- **Time rate:** A basic amount per hour is paid

Test your learning

1 Lara Binns works for Pole Potteries in both the throwing department and the baking department. Her employment agreement is that her basic week is 38 hours at a time rate of £9.60 per hour. Any overtime is at double the time rate.

During Week 39 Lara worked for 26 hours in the throwing department and 15 hours in the baking department. All of the overtime hours were due to a backlog in the throwing department.

Required

Show how the cost of employing Lara for Week 39 would be analysed for management accounting purposes using the table below.

	£
Basic wage	
Overtime	
Gross wage	
Cost centres	
Baking – labour	
Throwing – labour	
Total labour cost	

2 Cockerel Breakfast Cereals Limited pays a time rate of £7 per hour for a 35-hour week. Overtime is paid at time and a half for time worked in excess of 7 hours on weekdays, and double time for any work done at the weekend.

Required

Calculate the gross wage of the employees whose clock card information is summarised below and enter the details in the table on the following page.

	Hours worked			
	J. Sparrow	**K. Finch**	**M. Swallow**	**B. Cuckoo**
Monday	7	7	7.25	7
Tuesday	7	8	7	7
Wednesday	7.5	7	7.5	7
Thursday	8	8	7.5	7.5
Friday	7	7.5	7.5	7
Saturday	3		2	2

	J. Sparrow	K. Finch	M. Swallow	B. Cuckoo
Total hours				
	£	£	£	£
Basic wage				
Overtime: time and a half				
Overtime: double time				
Gross wage				

3 **Identify the labour payment method by putting a tick in the relevant column of the table below.**

Payment method	Time rate	Time rate plus bonus	Piecework	Differential piecework
Employees are paid for the hours worked and receive an incentive if a target is reached				
Employees are paid for output achieved and receive an incentive as production increases				
Employees are paid only for output achieved				
Employees are only paid for the hours worked				

Variances

7

Learning outcomes

3.1	Compare actual and budgeted costs and income
	• Calculate differences between actual and budgeted costs and income
	• Identify whether variance is adverse or favourable for costs and income
3.2	Apply exception reporting to identify significant variances
	• Calculate variances as a percentage of budget
	• Identify significant variances according to an organisation's policy
	• Report significant variances to a relevant manager

Assessment context

You should expect to see questions on this topic in every computer-based test.

Qualification context

Comparison of costs and income and variance analysis is also tested at an advanced level at levels 3 and 4.

Business context

All businesses want to control their costs by comparing their budgets with actual figures and trying to minimise the adverse variances. This allows them to achieve their business objectives and maximise their profits.

Chapter overview

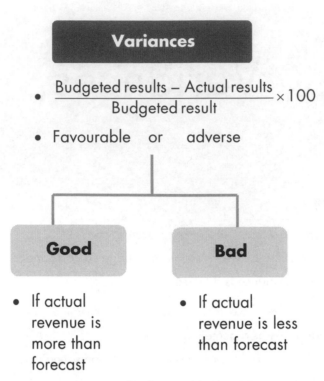

Variances

- $\dfrac{\text{Budgeted results} - \text{Actual results}}{\text{Budgeted result}} \times 100$

- Favourable   or   adverse

Good

- If actual revenue is more than forecast

Bad

- If actual revenue is less than forecast

Introduction

In the first chapter we considered the role of management in an organisation and that one of the key elements of this role was control. One way in which the costs and income of an organisation can be controlled is by comparing actual results with expected results as set out in the organisation's **budget**.

Deciding on what we expect to be the income and cost figures for a future period is a complex process which you will learn more about later in your studies. Many organisations have what is known as a **standard cost** for items they produce, setting out what they expect each unit to cost in terms of materials and labour. This standard cost is then multiplied by the number of items expected to be produced in order to estimate expected figures. Some organisations also have a standard for the selling price that they use in the calculations of income.

1 The budget

The budget of a business is its formal financial plan. The budget is determined for a future period and shows the expected levels of production and sales and the expected (or standard) costs and income associated with the production and sales levels.

Budgets are normally prepared on a monthly basis, so for each month's actual figures there will be budgeted or expected figures to compare with. The organisation as a whole is likely to have a budget for at least one year ahead, which is updated and reviewed regularly.

2 Comparing actual with budget

2.1 Variances

Comparison of expected figures with actual results is an extremely important tool for management in their control of the business. The differences between the actual costs and income and the budgeted costs and income are known as **variances**. These can be adverse ('bad' for the business) or favourable ('good' for the business).

Variance = budgeted result – actual result

> **√? Formula to learn**
>
> $$\% \text{ variance} = \frac{\text{Budgeted result} - \text{Actual result}}{\text{Budgeted result}} \times 100\%$$

Any significant variances should be reported to management as a priority, as the reasons for them must be investigated and corrective action taken.

2.2 Calculation of variances

Adverse variance – Where it is bad or negative for the business because:

- The actual cost is greater than the budgeted cost; or
- The actual income is less than the budgeted income.

Favourable variance – Where it is good or positive for the business because:

- The actual cost is less than budgeted cost; or
- The actual income is greater than budgeted income.

Illustration 1 Calculating variances

We have Wilmshurst's cost centre costs for December 20X6 from Chapter 3.

Code	Opening balance £	Update £	Closing balance 31 Dec 20X6 £
010101	37,886.98	604.00	38,490.98
010102	86,779.20	275.20	87,054.40
010103	23,556.90	4,345.48	27,902.38
010201	9,667.23		9,667.23
010202	93,674.55	103.20	93,777.75
010203	25,634.01	2,340.54	27,974.55
010301	10,356.35	44.00	10,400.35
010302	68,362.00		68,362.00
010303	12,563.98	1,550.00	14,113.98

From the budget, the expected costs for December 20X6 were as follows:

Budgeted costs – production cost centres – December 20X6

Code	£
010101	37,200.00
010102	86,770.00
010103	23,550.00
010201	9,600.00
010202	99,540.00
010203	32,600.00
010301	10,350.00
010302	74,300.00
010303	10,560.00

Now we need to compare the actual costs with the expected costs and to calculate the variances. This is done simply by deducting the actual figure from the budgeted figure.

Comparison of actual cost with budgeted cost for December 20X6

		Actual £	Budget £	Variance £
Cutting	Materials	38,490.98	37,200.00	−1,290.98 A
	Labour	87,054.40	86,770.00	−284.40 A
	Expenses	27,902.38	23,550.00	−4,352.38 A
Assembly	Materials	9,667.23	9,600.00	−67.23 A
	Labour	93,777.75	99,540.00	5,762.25 F
	Expenses	27,974.55	32,600.00	4,625.45 F
Polishing	Materials	10,400.35	10,350.00	−50.35 A
	Labour	68,362.00	74,300.00	5,938.00 F
	Expenses	14,113.98	10,560.00	−3,553.98 A

As these are all cost variances, it follows that:

- A negative result from deducting actual cost from budget is bad for the business – more cost has been incurred than planned. We can therefore classify such a result as adverse (A).

- A positive result is good for the business as it means less cost has been incurred than planned, so this is favourable (F).

Comparison of actual income with budgeted income

If we were dealing with income, the situation would be reversed.

- A positive result from deducting actual income from budgeted income is bad for the business, as less actual income has been generated than budgeted. This would be classified as adverse (A).

- A negative result is good for the business as it means more income has been generated than planned, so this is favourable (F).

Assessment focus point

An assessment question may give you a list of budgeted sales and costs and actual sales and costs and ask you to calculate the variances and indicate whether they are adverse or favourable.

Activity 1: Variances example 1

Lariss Ltd has the following budgeted and actual income and raw materials, labour, rent and electricity costs:

	Budget £	Actual £
Sales revenue	85,320	86,070
Raw materials		
Wood	8,250	7,500
Metal	6,720	6,900
Paint	2,185	2,300
Labour	15,660	16,530
Rent	30,000	31,500
Electricity	10,300	9,900
Total costs	73,115	74,630
Profit	12,205	11,440

Lariss Ltd only investigates variances which are of 5% significance or more.

Required

(a) **Calculate the variance for sales revenue and each line of cost.**

(b) **State whether the variance is favourable or adverse.**

(c) **Calculate the percentage of the budgeted cost that each variance represents.**

(d) **State which variances would require further investigation.**

(e) **State who might be interested in the paint variance.**

(f) **State what might have caused the wood variance.**

Use the following table to answer the above questions.

	Budget £	Actual £	(a) Variance £	(b) Favourable /Adverse	(c) Variance %
Sales revenue	85,320	86,070			
Raw materials					
Wood	8,250	7,500			
Metal	6,720	6,900			
Paint	2,185	2,300			
Labour	15,660	16,530			
Rent	30,000	31,500			
Electricity	10,300	9,900			
Total costs	73,115	74,630			
Profit	12,205	11,440			

(d)

(e)

(f)

Activity 2: Variances example 2

Identify whether the statements in the following table are true or false by ticking the appropriate column.

Statement	True	False
An adverse cost variance is where budgeted costs are greater than actual costs		
When budgeted sales revenue is greater than actual sales revenue, there is a favourable sales variance		
A favourable cost variance occurs when an actual cost of £6,000 is compared to a budgeted cost of £10 per unit for a budgeted output of 550 units		

2.3 Reporting variances

Normally the managers of a business only wish to be informed about significant variances, by means of a **variance report** or **significance report**.

The significance of a variance cannot be determined simply by its size – the size of the variance must be compared with the budgeted amount. For example, a variance of £10,000 is tiny if the budgeted amount is £1,000,000 but is huge if the budgeted amount is only £15,000.

Therefore the significance of a variance will often be determined by measuring it as a percentage of the budgeted figure. If it is more than, say, 10% of the budgeted amount then the organisation's policy may be that it must be reported to management.

Illustration 2 Reporting variances

This illustration follows on from Illustration 1.

We will now calculate the percentage that each variance is of the **budgeted** amount. Note that:

- It is calculated relative to the budgeted or expected amount, **not** the actual amount

- You can ignore any minus sign as it is the relative size of the figures that are key here

Cutting –	Materials	1,290.98/37,200	×	100	=	3.5% A
	Labour	284.40/86,770	×	100	=	0.3% A
	Expenses	4,352.38/23,550	×	100	=	18.5% A
Assembly –	Materials	67.23/9,600	×	100	=	0.7% A
	Labour	5,762.25/99,540	×	100	=	5.8% F
	Expenses	4,625.45/32,600	×	100	=	14.2% F
Polishing –	Materials	50.35/10,350	×	100	=	0.5% A
	Labour	5,938.00/74,300	×	100	=	8.0% F
	Expenses	3,553.98/10,560	×	100	=	33.7% A

If Wilmshurst's policy is to report any variances over 5% of the budgeted amount then the following would be reported:

Cutting –	Expenses	£4,352.38 Adverse
Assembly –	Labour	£5,762.25 Favourable
	Expenses	£4,625.45 Favourable
Polishing –	Labour	£5,938.00 Favourable
	Expenses	£3,553.98 Adverse

If the policy had been to report only variances greater than 10% of budget then the only variances reported would have been the three expenses variances.

Assessment focus point

An assessment question may ask you to calculate variances as a percentage of budget.

You might also be asked in an assessment to identify who you should report a significant variance to. The following table illustrates areas of income and costs and the managers who are responsible for them:

Income or cost	Manager responsible
Income	Sales manager
Materials	Purchasing manager Production manager
Labour	Production manager Human resources manager
Expenses	Administration manager

Activity 3: Variances as a percentage

The ledger accounts of Spelprint show actual costs and revenues for the month of December 20X0.

Required

Complete Spelprint's monthly comparison schedules. In the column headed 'Difference (£)', enter the monetary amount of the difference between actual and forecast totals for December 20X0, using the symbol '+' to indicate an increase over forecast and the symbol '-' to indicate a decrease compared with forecast.

In the column headed 'Difference (%)' enter each difference as a percentage of the forecast total, again using the symbols '+' and '-' and expressing the percentages to one decimal place.

Spelprint Limited Monthly comparison schedule Month: December 20X0					
Account code	Account name	Actual £	Forecast £	Difference £	Difference %
100–500	Mannheim Publishing: books	11,550	12,000		
200–500	Bigbooks plc: books	11,250	10,000		
300–600	Media Magic: advertising	5,352	5,500		
300–700	Media Magic: other jobs	3,180	3,000		
400–500	Other customers: books	7,120	8,000		
400–700	Other customers: other jobs	22,349	20,000		
810–910	Direct materials: paper	5,750	6,000		
810–920	Direct materials: card	5,419	5,000		
810–930	Direct materials: ink	2,895	3,000		
820–940	Employee costs: gross pay	9,960	10,000		
820–950	Employee costs: employer NIC	987	1,100		
830–960	Accountancy and legal costs	482	500		

Chapter summary

- One of the key roles of management is control – this can be helped by constant comparison of actual results with expected or budgeted figures.

- A key element in management control of a business is the budget – actual results should be compared with the expected or budgeted figures and the differences, called variances, reported to management when significant.

- It is important that both adverse and favourable variances are reported on a significance basis, as a percentage of the budgeted figure.

Keywords

- **Adverse variance:** The actual result is worse for the business than the budgeted result

- **Budget:** Formalised financial plan of the future operations of the organisation

- **Favourable variance:** The actual result is better for the business than the budgeted result

- **Standard cost:** An estimate of materials and labour cost per unit to use when developing an estimate of future results

- **Variance report** or **significance report:** A report to an appropriate person of significant variances between actual and budget, usually identified as being above a certain percentage of budget

- **Variances:** The difference between the expected or budgeted cost/income and the actual cost/income

Test your learning

1   Given below are the actual costs of the production cost centres for Pole Potteries for November 20X6.

		£
Throwing	Materials	12,140
	Labour	7,440
	Expenses	6,330
Baking	Materials	1,330
	Labour	2,440
	Expenses	10,490
Painting	Materials	4,260
	Labour	13,570
	Expenses	2,680

Here are the budgeted costs for the production cost centres for Pole Potteries for November 20X6.

		£
Throwing	Materials	11,200
	Labour	6,150
	Expenses	7,130
Baking	Materials	1,500
	Labour	2,490
	Expenses	11,350
Painting	Materials	3,660
	Labour	11,240
	Expenses	2,800

Required

Produce a comparison of actual costs for November 20X6 with budgeted costs for the month and show the amount of the variances and whether each one is adverse (A) or favourable (F). Fill in your answers in the table below. The policy of Pole Potteries is to report any variances that are more than 10% of the budgeted amount to management. Calculate the variance as a percentage of budget for each cost. Enter your answers in the following table.

	Actual £	Budget £	Variance £
Throwing			
Materials			
Labour			
Expenses			
Baking			
Materials			
Labour			
Expenses			
Painting			
Materials			
Labour			
Expenses			

Cost centre	Expense	Variance £	Variance as a % of budget
Throwing	Materials		
	Labour		
	Expenses		
Baking	Materials		
	Labour		
	Expenses		
Painting	Materials		
	Labour		
	Expenses		

2 **Identify the following statements as being true or false by putting a tick in the relevant column of the table below.**

Statement	True	False
The difference between a budgeted and an actual cost is called performance		
An adverse variance occurs when actual income exceeds budgeted income		

3 A business has produced a variance report detailing budgeted and actual costs for the month.

Required

Calculate the variance for each cost type and then determine whether it is adverse or favourable by putting a tick in the relevant column of the table below.

Cost type	Budget £	Actual £	Variance £	Adverse	Favourable
Materials	52,480	51,940			
Labour	65,920	67,370			
Production overheads	34,340	35,680			
Selling and distribution overheads	10,270	12,840			
Administration overheads	11,560	10,470			

4 The following variance report for a particular month has been produced for a business. Any variance in excess of 5% of budget is deemed to be significant and should be reported to management.

Required

Calculate the variances in the table below as a percentage of the budgeted figure and indicate whether they are significant or not by putting a tick in the relevant column.

Cost type	Budget £	Variance £	Adverse/ Favourable	Variance as a % of budget	Significant	Not significant
Materials	134,280	20,390	Favourable			
Labour	128,410	5,400	Adverse			
Production overheads	87,360	9,280	Adverse			
Selling and distribution overheads	52,400	1,200	Adverse			
Administration overheads	32,420	4,580	Favourable			

Activity answers

CHAPTER 1 Introduction to costing systems

Activity 1: Types of business 1

☑ Partnership

A partnership, as it is owned and run by three people.

Activity 2: Types of business 2

☑ Limited company

Limited company as the shareholders of ABC Ltd have limited liability to the extent of the amount paid on their shares.

Activity 3: Revenue or capital expenditure

Transaction	Capital	Revenue
Purchase of building for £1m	✓	
Purchase of goods for resale £50,000		✓
Payment of wages £25,000		✓
Purchase of materials for £75,000 to manufacture goods for resale		✓
Purchase of van for £15,000	✓	

Activity 4: Financial and cost accounting

Characteristic	Financial accounting	Cost accounting
This system produces annual financial statements	✓	
The statements from this system are used to estimate the cost of producing a product or providing a service		✓
The statements from this system are used to assist management in planning, control and decision making		✓
This system produces statements for external users	✓	

CHAPTER 2 Cost classification

Activity 1: Classification by function

	Production costs	Administration costs	Selling and distribution	Financing costs
Purchase of plastic and rubber material	✓			
Rental of finished goods warehouse			✓	
Depreciation of its own fleet of delivery vehicles			✓	
Commission paid to sales staff			✓	
Insurance of office furniture		✓		
Interest paid on loan				✓

Activity 2: Classification by element

Cost	Material	Labour	Overhead
Insurance of factory			✓
Plastic used in the production of packaging	✓		
Wages paid to employees		✓	
Rent of office space			✓
Training costs for factory workers			✓

CHAPTER 3 Coding costs

Activity 1: Coding of costs

Medieval Castle

Nos	Invoices	Invoice £	Code
123	Retail staff salaries	20,000	R02
124	Costumes for tour guides	489	T05
125	Garden forks	150	G05
126	Electricity bill for Medieval Castle	3,598	X04
127	Rental of café building	1,843	C06
128	Retail shop telephone bill	317	R01
129	Gardening clothes	271	G05
130	Miniature castles for resale	52	R03
131	Payroll costs	2,000	X02
132	Walking sticks for resale to walkers	229	R03
133	Tea, coffee and fresh cream cakes	99	C03

Activity 2: Coding transactions

Data entry sheet: purchase invoices

Date 20X0	Supplier	Details of purchase	Amount £	Cost centre code	Cost category
8 Jan	Acorn Mills Limited	Paper for printing jobs	971.50	810	910
8 Jan	Thorn & Co	Accountancy services	275.00	830	960
8 Jan	Parslow Limited	Lubricants	322.72	830	970
8 Jan	Maxwell Smith	Ink for printing jobs	194.00	810	930
8 Jan	Rimmer Limited	Paper for printing jobs	513.81	810	910

Activity 3: Coding transactions continued

Coding sheets: salaries for the month of December 20X0

Description	Amount	Accounts code	
	£	Cost centre	Cost category
Gross pay	9960.00	820	940
Employer NIC	986.81	820	950

Activity 4: Investment centre coding

Activity	Code	Nature of cost	Sub-code	Transaction	Code
Investments	IN	External	200	Internal investment funds	IN220
		Internal	220	Salaries of project staff	CO500
Revenues	RE	UK	300	Overseas revenue arising from project	RE330
		Overseas	330	Materials used on project	CO400
Costs	CO	Material	400	Bank loan raised for investment in the project	IN200
		Labour	500	Sales to UK customers	RE300
		Overheads	600		

CHAPTER 4 Cost behaviour

Activity 1: Fixed cost per unit

Output level (units)	Fixed cost per bench £
1,000	20
10,000	2
20,000	1
100,000	0.20

Activity 2: Fixed or variable cost

Costs	Fixed	Variable
Leasing costs of the boat building yard	✓	
Paint and varnish		✓
Designer's salary	✓	
Material for sails		✓
Insurance for the boat building yard	✓	

Activity 3: Fixed, variable or semi-variable cost

Cost	Fixed	Variable	Semi-variable
Employees in the factory paid on a piecework basis (per car produced)		✓	
Hire of specialist tuning equipment, consisting of a monthly payment plus a usage charge			✓
Yearly payment for design costs	✓		
Metal used in the manufacture of the cars		✓	

Activity 4: Costs at different levels of production

Statement	Fixed	Variable	Semi-variable
At 6,000 units, this cost is £21,000, and at 8,750 units, it is £30,625		✓	
At 4,000 units, this cost is £5.00 per unit, and at 5,000 units it is £4.00 per unit	✓		
At 9,000 units this cost is £45,500, and at 11,000 units, this cost is £51,500			✓

Activity 5: Unit cost

Element	Unit product cost £
Materials	8
Labour	3
Direct cost	11
Overheads	10
Total	21

Activity 6: High–low method 1

Fixed cost = | £12,000 |

Output (units)		Total cost £
Highest	4,200	54,000
Lowest	2,900	41,000
High-low	1,300	13,000

$$\text{Variable cost per unit} = \frac{\text{High cost} - \text{Low cost}}{\text{High output} - \text{Low output}}$$
$$= \frac{£13,000}{1,300}$$
$$= £10$$

At 4,200 units

	£
Total cost	54,000
Less variable cost (4,200 × £10)	42,000
= fixed cost	12,000

Or, at 2,900 units

	£
Total cost	41,000
Less variable cost (2,900 × £10)	29,000
= fixed cost	12,000

Activity 7: High–low method 2

£	6,000 units	7,500 units	8,000 units
Variable cost		67,500	
Fixed cost		43,000	
Total cost	97,000	110,500	115,000

Workings

Output (units)		Total cost £
Highest	8,000	115,000
Lowest	6,000	97,000
High-Low	2,000	18,000

$$\text{Variable cost per unit} = \frac{\text{High cost} - \text{Low cost}}{\text{High output} - \text{Low output}}$$

$$= \frac{£18,000}{2,000}$$

$$= £9$$

At 8,000 units

	£
Total cost	115,000
Less variable cost (8,000 × £9)	72,000
= fixed cost	43,000

So, at 7,500 units

	£
Fixed cost	43,000
Variable cost (7,500 × £9)	67,500
Total cost	110,500

Activity 1: Closing inventory values

(a) **FIFO method**

Date	Receipts Quantity	Cost per unit £	Total cost £	Issues Quantity	Cost per unit £	Total cost £	Balance Quantity	Total cost £
1 Mar	100	2.00	200				100	200
2 Mar	300	2.10	630				400	830
5 Mar				50	2.00	100	350	730
17 Mar	100	2.30	230				450	960
20 Mar				50	2.00	100	300 (W1)	650
				100	2.10	210		
				150		310		

W1 (100 @ £2.30) + (200 @ £2.10) = £650

LIFO method

Date	Receipts Quantity	Cost per unit £	Total cost £	Issues Quantity	Cost per unit £	Total cost £	Balance Quantity	Total cost £
1 Mar	100	2.00	200				100	200
2 Mar	300	2.10	630				400	830
5 Mar				50	2.10	105	350	725
17 Mar	100	2.30	230				450	955
20 Mar				100	2.30	230	300 (W2)	620
				50	2.10	105		
				150		335		

W2 (200 @ £2.10) + (100 @ £2.00) = £620

AVCO method

Date	Receipts Quantity	Receipts Cost per unit £	Receipts Total cost £	Issues Quantity	Issues Cost per unit £	Issues Total cost £	Balance Quantity	Balance Total cost £	Balance Avg. cost £
1 Mar	100	2.00	200				100	200	2.00
2 Mar	300	2.10	630				400	830	2.075
5 Mar				50	2.075	103.75	350	726.25	2.075
17 Mar	100	2.30	230				450	956.25	2.125
20 Mar				150	2.125	318.75	300	637.50	2.125

(b)

FIFO		LIFO		AVCO	
Sales revenue	1,000	Sales revenue	1,000	Sales revenue	1,000
200u × £5/u		200u × £5/u		200u × £5/u	
Less cost of sales		Less cost of sales		Less cost of sales	
Issues @ (100 + 310)	410	Issues @ (105 + 335)	440	Issues @ 103.75 + 318.75	422.50
Gross profit	590	Gross profit	560	Gross profit	577.50

Activity 2: Identifying inventory valuation methods 1

	FIFO	LIFO	AVCO
Costs issues of inventory at the most recent purchase price		✓	
Costs issues of inventory at the oldest purchase price	✓		
Values closing inventory at the most recent purchase price	✓		
Closing inventory is valued at the average of the cost of purchases			✓

Activity 3: Identifying inventory valuation methods 2

Statement	FIFO	LIFO	AVCO
The closing inventory is valued at £7,200	✓		
The issue of 1,800 units is costed at £10,800		✓	
The issue of 1,800 units is costed at £10,200			✓

Activity 4: Identifying inventory valuation methods 3

Statement	True	False
AVCO values the closing inventory at £6,800	✓	
FIFO costs the issue of 1,800 units at £12,800		✓
LIFO values the closing inventory at £6,200	✓	

Note that FIFO values the issue at £9,800.

Activity 5: Cost of issues and inventory valuation

Method	Cost of issue on March 20 £	Closing inventory at March 31 £
FIFO	4,100 (700 @ £5 = £3,500 100 @ £6 = £600)	7,300 (500 @ £6 = £3,000 200 @ £8 = £1,600 300 @ £9 = £2,700)
LIFO	5,200 (200 @ £8 = £1,600) 600 @ £6 = £3,600	6,200 (700 @ £5 = £3,500) 300 @ £9 = 2,700
AVCO	4,640 (800 @ £5.80 £5.80 being £8,700/1,500)	6,760 (700 @ £5.80 add 300 @ £9 = 1,000 @£6.76 = £6,760)

Activity 6: Cost of goods sold

Direct material used   £ | 51,300

Cost of goods manufactured   £ | 132,100

Direct cost   £ | 115,700

Cost of goods sold   £ | 130,500

Manufacturing cost   £ | 130,200

Workings

	£
Opening raw materials inventory	12,500
+ raw materials purchases	47,000
– closing inventory of raw materials	(8,200)
Direct materials used	51,300
+ direct labour costs	64,400
Direct cost	115,700
+ manufacturing overhead costs	14,500
Manufacturing cost	130,200
+ opening inventory of WIP	4,700
– closing inventory of WIP	(2,800)
Cost of goods manufactured	132,100
+ opening inventory of finished goods	27,600
– closing inventory of finished goods	(29,200)
= COST OF GOODS SOLD	130,500

CHAPTER 6 Labour costs and overheads

Activity 1: Normal time and overtime 1

	Hours	Rate per hour	£
Normal time	35	4	140
Overtime	5	6	30
Total			170

Activity 2: Normal time and overtime 2

Employee	Hours worked	Basic wage £	Overtime £	Gross wage £
Y. Sterling	42	320	24	344
T. Bindon	46	320	72	392

Activity 3: Net pay calculation

	Hours		Rate per hour	£
Basic pay	42	×	£6	252.00
Overtime premium	2	×	(£6 × 0.5)	6.00
Gross pay				258.00
PAYE	258.00	×	25%	(64.50)
Employees' NIC	258.00		10%	(25.80)
NET PAY				167.70

Activity 4: Piecework pay 1

£690

		£
First 100 units	(100 × £4)	400
Next 50 units	(50 × £4.50)	225
Remaining 13 units	(13 × £5)	65
Week 48 pay		690

Activity 5: Piecework pay 2

Statement	True	False
Employees' pay will remain the same if more units are produced		✓
An employee is paid 40p per unit and earns £340 for a production of 850 units	✓	
An employee who is paid £420 for a production of 700 units is paid 60p per unit	✓	
Employees' pay will decrease if less units are produced	✓	

Activity 6: Time based pay plus bonus and piecework pay

Hours worked	Unit output	Basic wage £	Bonus £	Gross wage £	Piecework wage £
30	400	300	0	300	400
40	660	400	30	430	660

Activity 7: Time based pay plus bonus

Statement	True	False
During a 40-hour week an employee produces 820 units and does not receive a bonus		✓
During a 36-hour week an employee produces 750 units and receives a bonus of £15	✓	
During a 42-hour week an employee produces 900 units and receives total pay of £450	✓	

Activity 8: Direct and indirect labour cost

	Hours	Rate/hour	Direct cost £	Indirect cost £
Skilled workers				
Basic pay (normal hours)	35	£10 × 7	2,450	0
Basic pay (general overtime)	30	£10	300	0
Specific overtime	20	£10 × 1.5	300	0
Overtime premium (general overtime)	30	£10 × 0.5	0	150
Semi-skilled workers				
Basic pay (normal hours)	35	£7.50 × 4	0	1,050
Specific overtime	10	£7.50 × 1.5	112.50	0
General overtime	10	£7.50 × 1.5	0	112.50
			3,162.50	1,312.50

Activity 9: Overhead absorption rate

	Machine hour	Labour hour	Unit
Overheads (£)	500,000	500,000	500,000
Activity	35,000	20,000	58,000
Absorption rate (£)	14.29	25.00	8.62

CHAPTER 7 Variances

Activity 1: Variances example 1

(a)–(c)

	Budget £	Actual £	(a) Variance £	(b) Favourable /Adverse	(c) Variance %
Sales revenue	85,320	86,070	750	F	0.9
Raw materials					

	Budget £	Actual £	(a) Variance £	(b) Favourable /Adverse	(c) Variance %
Wood	8,250	7,500	750	F	9.1
Metal	6,720	6,900	180	A	2.7
Paint	2,185	2,300	115	A	5.3
Labour	15,660	16,530	870	A	5.6
Rent	30,000	31,500	1,500	A	5.0
Electricity	10,300	9,900	400	F	3.9
Total costs	73,115	74,630	1,515	A	2.1
Profit	12,205	11,440	765	A	6.3

(d) Further investigation required for:
- Wood
- Paint
- Labour
- Rent costs

(e) • The purchasing department Perhaps a cheaper supplier could be found.

   • The production department Perhaps there is a lot of wastage resulting in more paint than necessary being purchased.

(f) • Cheaper supplier found
   • Bulk buying resulting in discounts
   • Less wood required in production due to reduced wastage

Activity 2: Variances example 2

Statement	True	False
An adverse cost variance is where budgeted costs are greater than actual costs		✓
When budgeted sales revenue is greater than actual sales revenue, there is a favourable sales variance		✓
A favourable cost variance occurs when an actual cost of £6,000 is compared to a budgeted cost of £10 per unit for a budgeted output of 550 units		✓

Activity 3: Variances as a percentage

Spelprint Limited Monthly comparison schedule Month: December 20X0					
Account code	Account name	Actual £	Forecast £	Difference £	Difference %
100-500	Mannheim Publishing: books	11,550	12,000	–450	–3.8
200-500	Bigbooks plc: books	11,250	10,000	+1,250	+12.5
300-600	Media Magic: advertising	5,352	5,500	–148	–2.7
300-700	Media Magic: other jobs	3,180	3,000	+180	+6.0
400-500	Other customers: books	7,120	8,000	–880	–11.0
400-700	Other customers: other jobs	22,349	20,000	+2,349	+11.7
810-910	Direct materials: paper	5,750	6,000	–250	–4.2
810-920	Direct materials: card	5,419	5,000	+419	+8.4
810-930	Direct materials: ink	2,895	3,000	–105	–3.5
820-940	Employee costs: gross pay	9,960	10,000	–40	–0.4
820-950	Employee costs: employer NIC	987	1,100	–113	–10.3
830-960	Accountancy and legal costs	482	500	–18	–3.6

Test your learning: answers

Chapter 1

1

Transaction	Cash	Credit
Purchase of a van with payment agreed in one month		✓
Sale of goods paid for by credit card	✓	
Purchase of printer paper accompanied by an invoice		✓
Sale of goods paid for by cheque	✓	
Purchase of printer paper by cheque	✓	

2

Transaction	Capital	Revenue
Purchase of a computer for resale to a customer by a computer retailer		✓
Purchase of a computer by a computer retailer for use in the sales office	✓	
Payment of wages by an accounting firm		✓
Purchase of a building by a property developer to serve as head office	✓	

3

	Statement of profit or loss	Statement of financial position
Sales revenue	✓	
Non-current assets		✓
Expenses	✓	
Current assets		✓
Profit or loss	✓	

4

Characteristic	Financial accounting	Cost accounting
It helps with decision making inside the business		✓
Its end product consists of statements for external publication	✓	
It focuses on costs		✓
It focuses on asset valuations	✓	

Chapter 2

1

Cost	Materials	Labour	Overheads
Metal used for casing	✓		
Business rates on warehouse			✓
Wages of operatives in assembly department		✓	
Salary of factory supervisor		✓	

2

Cost	Direct	Indirect
Detergent used for cleaning floors	✓	
Depreciation of vacuum cleaner		✓
Wages of bookings assistant		✓
Wages of cleaners	✓	

3

Cost	Production	Selling and distribution	Administration
Purchases of sand	✓		
Fuel for salesperson's vehicle		✓	
Printer paper for office			✓
Wages of factory workers	✓		

4

Cost	Production	Selling and distribution	Administration
Factory rent	✓		
Managing Director's salary			✓
Sales Director's salary		✓	
Depreciation charge on office equipment			✓
Depreciation charge on factory plant and equipment	✓		
Fuel for delivery vans		✓	
Factory heating and lighting	✓		

5

	Tick
Cost centre	
Profit centre	
Investment centre	✓

A manager of an investment centre has control over the costs, revenues and assets of the division.

A manager of a profit centre has control over costs and revenues but not assets.

A manager of a cost centre has control over the costs but not the revenues or the assets.

Chapter 3

1

INVOICE

Purbeck Clay
Granite Yard
Compston BH3 4TL
Tel 01929 464810
VAT Reg 1164 2810 67

To: Pole Potteries

Invoice number: 36411

Date/tax point: 16 Dec 20X6

Order number: 11663

Account number: SL 42

Quantity	Description	Inventory code	Unit amount £	Total £
50 kg	Throwing clay	TC412	6.80	111 340.00
10 litres	Paint - Fuchsia	PF67	2.80	131 28.00

Net total	368.00
VAT	73.60
Invoice total	441.60

Terms
Net 30 days
E & OE

2

	£	Code
Throwing – labour (23 hours @ £9.60) + (3 hours @ £9.60 × 2)	278.40	112
Baking – labour 15 hours @ £9.60	144.00	122
Throwing – expense – employer's NIC	26.42	113
Baking – expense – employer's NIC	15.25	123

3

	£	Code
Throwing – expense – rent £15,000 × 15%	2,250	
Throwing – expense – cleaning	200	
Throwing – total	2,450	113
Baking – expense – rent £15,000 × 40%	6,000	
Baking – expense – servicing	600	
Baking – total	6,600	123
Painting – expense – rent £15,000 × 15%	2,250	133
Packaging – expense – rent £5,000 × 20%	1,000	143
Stores – expense – rent £5,000 × 80%	4,000	153
Maintenance – expense – rent £15,000 × 10%	1,500	163
Selling and distribution – expense – rent £3,000 × 50%	1,500	
Selling and distribution – expense – advertising	400	
Selling and distribution – total	1,900	173
Canteen – expense – rent £15,000 × 20%	3,000	183
Administration – expense – rent £3,000 × 50%	1,500	193

4

Transaction	Code
Materials for casings	2/10
Sales to Paris, EU	1/20
Business rates on factory	2/20
Printing of marketing leaflets	3/20
Sales to Holmfirth, UK	1/10
Office stationery	4/20

5

Transaction	Code
Architect fees for project	COS700
Herbert Ltd money invested in project	INV200
Material used on project	COS500
Project revenue arising in Africa	REV400
Bank loan invested in project	INV100
Salaries paid to employees	COS600

Chapter 4

1   (a)   Total fixed cost

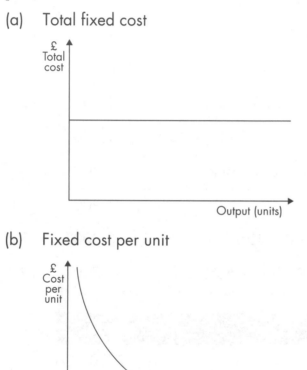

    (b)   Fixed cost per unit

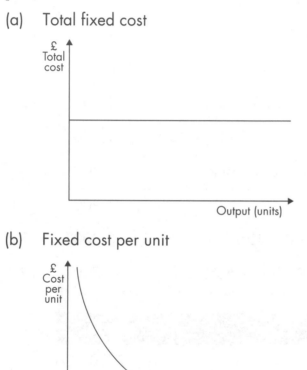

2

Cost	Fixed	Variable	Semi-variable
Entertainment budget for the year	✓		
Telephone costs that include a fixed line rental charge plus call charges			✓
Leather used in the production process		✓	
Labour costs paid as production overtime		✓	

3

Statement	True	False
Total variable costs do not change directly with changes in activity but variable costs per unit do		✓
Fixed costs per unit decrease with increasing levels of output	✓	

4

Statement	Fixed	Variable	Semi-variable
Costs of £4 per unit at 30,000 units and £24 per unit at 5,000 units (working 1)	✓		
Costs of £50,000 are made up of a fixed charge of £20,000 and a further cost of £10 per unit at 3,000 units			✓
Costs are £60,000 at 12,000 units and £35,000 at 7,000 units (working 2)		✓	

Workings

1   30,000 × £4 = £120,000; 5,000 × £24 = £120,000. The total cost remains the same so this is a fixed cost.

2   £60,000/12,000 = £5.00 per unit; £35,000/7,000 = £5.00 per unit. The cost per unit remains the same so this is a variable cost.

£	6,500 units	12,000 units	13,500 units
Variable cost		24,000	
Fixed cost		4,500	
Total cost	17,500	28,500	31,500

Workings

Output (units)		Total cost £
Highest	13,500	31,500
Lowest	6,500	17,500
High–low	7,000	14,000

$$\text{Variable cost per unit} = \frac{\text{High cost} - \text{Low cost}}{\text{High output} - \text{Low output}}$$

$$= \frac{£14,000}{7,000}$$

$$= £2$$

At 6,500 units

	£
Total cost	17,500
Less variable cost (6,500 × £2)	13,000
= fixed cost	4,500

Using the fixed cost of £4,500, and the variable cost of £2 per unit, we can now estimate the total cost at 12,000 units:

	£
Fixed cost	4,500
Add variable cost (12,000 × £2)	24,000
Total cost	28,500

Chapter 5

1

	Raw materials	WIP	Finished goods
Bricks at a brick-making factory			✓
Bricks in stores at a building company	✓		
The ingredients for making bricks held in stores at a brick-making company	✓		
A brick that has been moulded but not fired in the kiln at a brick-making factory		✓	

2 (a) **FIFO**

Stores Ledger Account								
	Receipts			Issues			Balance	
Date	Quantity (kg)	Cost per kg £	Value £	Quantity (kg)	Cost per kg £	Value £	Quantity (kg)	Value £
3 Jan							100	880
16 Jan	400	9.00	3,600				500	4,480
27 Jan				100	8.80	880		
				150	9.00	1,350		
				250		2,230	250	2,250
5 Feb				180	9.00	1,620	70	630
9 Feb	400	9.30	3,720				470	4,350
17 Feb				70	9.00	630		
				350	9.30	3,255		
				420		3,885	50	465
25 Feb	500	9.35	4,675				550	5,140

Cost of material issues   = £2,230 + £1,620 + £3,885

           = £7,735

Value of closing inventory   = £5,140

(b) **LIFO**

| | Stores Ledger Account | | | | | | | |
| | Receipts | | | Issues | | | Balance | |
Date	Quantity (kg)	Cost per kg £	Value £	Quantity (kg)	Cost per kg £	Value £	Quantity (kg)	Value £
3 Jan							100	880
16 Jan	400	9.00	3,600				500	4,480
27 Jan				250	9.00	2,250	250	2,230
5 Feb				150	9.00	1,350		
				30	8.80	264		
				180		1,614	70	616
9 Feb	400	9.30	3,720				470	4,336
17 Feb				400	9.30	3,720		
				20	8.80	176		
				420		3,896	50	440
25 Feb	500	9.35	4,675				550	5,115

Cost of material issues = £2,250 + £1,614 + £3,896

= £7,760

Value of closing inventory = £5,115

(c) **AVCO**

	Receipts			Issues			Balance	
Date	**Quantity (kg)**	**Cost per kg £**	**Value £**	**Quantity (kg)**	**Cost per kg £**	**Value £**	**Quantity (kg)**	**Value £**
3 Jan							100	880.00
16 Jan	400	9.00	3,600				500	4,480.00
27 Jan				250	8.96	2,240.00	250	2,240.00
5 Feb				180	8.96	1,612.80	70	627.20
9 Feb	400	9.30	3,720				470	4,347.20
17 Feb				420	9.25	3,885.00	50	462.20
25 Feb	500	9.35	4,675				550	5,137.20

Cost of material issues = £2,240.00 + £1,612.80 + £3,885.00

= £7,737.80

Value of closing inventory = £5,137.20

3

Statement	True	False
FIFO costs issues of inventory at the oldest purchase price	✓	
AVCO costs issues of inventory at the most recent purchase price		✓
LIFO costs issues of inventory at the most recent purchase price	✓	
FIFO values closing inventory at the oldest purchase price		✓
LIFO values closing inventory at the oldest purchase price	✓	
AVCO values closing inventory at an average purchase price	✓	

4

Method	Cost of issue on 11 Oct	Closing inventory at 31 Oct
FIFO	£162.00 (W1)	£958.00 (W2)
LIFO	£202.50 (W3)	£917.50 (W4)
AVCO	£180.00 (W5)	£940.00 (W6)

Workings

1   $90 \times £360/200 = £162.00$

2   $£160 + £240 + £360 + £360 - £162 = £958.00$

3   $90 \times £360/160 = £202.50$

4   $£160 + £240 + £360 + £360 - £202.50 = £917.50$

5   $(£360 + £360)/(200 + 160) = £2$ per item, so the issue is $£2 \times 90 = £180.00$

6   $£240 + £160 + £360 + £360 - £180 = £940.00$

Chapter 6

1

	£
Basic wage 38 hours @ £9.60	364.80
Overtime 3 hours @ £9.60 × 2	57.60
Gross wage (26 + 15 = 41 hours)	422.40
Cost centres	
Baking – labour 15 hours @ £9.60	144.00
Throwing – labour (23 hours @ £9.60) + (3 hours @ £9.60 × 2)	278.40
Total labour cost	422.40

2

	J. Sparrow	K. Finch	M. Swallow	B. Cuckoo
Total hours	39.5	37.5	38.75	37.5
Basic wage (35 × £7)	£245.00	£245.00	£245.00	£245.00
Overtime: time and a half	(1.5 × £7 × 1.5)	(2.5 × £7 × 1.5)	(1.75 × £7 × 1.5)	(0.5 × £7 × 1.5)
	= £15.75	= £26.25	= £18.38	= £5.25
Overtime: double time	(3 × £7 × 2)		(2 × £7 × 2)	(2 × £7 × 2)
	= £42.00		= £28.00	= £28.00
Gross wage	£302.75	£271.25	£291.38	£278.25

3

Payment method	Time rate	Time rate plus bonus	Piecework	Differential piecework
Employees are paid for the hours worked and receive an incentive if a target is reached		✓		
Employees are paid for output achieved and receive an incentive as production increases				✓
Employees are paid only for output achieved			✓	
Employees are only paid for the hours worked	✓			

Chapter 7

1   **Comparison of November 20X6 cost centre costs with budget**

	Actual £	Budget £	Variance £
Throwing			
Materials	12,140	11,200	940 A
Labour	7,440	6,150	1,290 A
Expenses	6,330	7,130	800 F
Baking			
Materials	1,330	1,500	170 F
Labour	2,440	2,490	50 F
Expenses	10,490	11,350	860 F
Painting			
Materials	4,260	3,660	600 A
Labour	13,570	11,240	2,330 A
Expenses	2,680	2,800	120 F

Cost centre	Expense	Variance £	Variance as a % of budget
Throwing	Materials	940 A	8.4
	Labour	1,290 A	21.0
	Expenses	800 F	11.2
Baking	Materials	170 F	11.3
	Labour	50 F	2.0
	Expenses	860 F	7.6
Painting	Materials	600 A	16.4
	Labour	2,330 A	20.7
	Expenses	120 F	4.3

2

Statement	True	False
The difference between a budgeted and an actual cost is called performance		✓
An adverse variance occurs when actual income exceeds budgeted income		✓

3

Cost type	Budget £	Actual £	Variance £	Adverse	Favourable
Materials	52,480	51,940	540		✓
Labour	65,920	67,370	1,450	✓	
Production overheads	34,340	35,680	1,340	✓	
Selling and distribution overheads	10,270	12,840	2,570	✓	
Administration overheads	11,560	10,470	1,090		✓

4

Cost type	Budget £	Variance £	Adverse/Favourable	Variance as a % of budget	Significant	Not significant
Materials	134,280	20,390	Favourable	15.2	✓	
Labour	128,410	5,400	Adverse	4.2		✓
Production overheads	87,360	9,280	Adverse	10.6	✓	
Selling and distribution overheads	52,400	1,200	Adverse	2.3		✓
Administration overheads	32,420	4,580	Favourable	14.1	✓	

Synoptic assessment preparation

Certain *Elements of Costing* assessment objectives will be tested in the *AAT Foundation Certificate in Accounting* synoptic assessment. Therefore, at this stage in your studies, it is useful to consider the style of tasks you may see in the synoptic assessment.

However, it is recommended that the *AAT Foundation Certificate in Accounting* synoptic assessment is only taken when all other units have been completed.

Questions

1   Runn Ltd organises events such as road running and cycling races. The latest running race was budgeted to cost:

Water: £0.50 per person

Marshals: £60 per hundred people

1,200 runners entered the race. The actual costs are shown in the table below and you have been asked to compare these with the budgeted costs:

Required

Complete the table below by:

- **Inserting the total budgeted amount for each cost**
- **Inserting the variance for each cost**
- **Selecting whether each variance is adverse or favourable**

Race cost performance report				
Cost	Budget £	Actual £	Variance £	Adverse/ Favourable
Water		625		▼
Marshals		630		▼

Drop-down list:

Adverse

Favourable

2   Your manager has asked you to prepare a cost analysis at different levels of output for a product. You are told that fixed costs are £36,000 and variable costs are £3 per unit.

Required

Complete the table below to show fixed, variable and total and unit costs for each of the three levels of output, giving your answer to two decimal places.

Output	Fixed costs £	Variable costs £	Total costs £	Unit cost £
3,000 units				
8,000 units				
10,000 units				

3 **In the box below, write a short report for non-finance staff containing:**

- **An explanation of variances**
- **An explanation of significance of variances**

Solutions

1

	Race cost performance report			
Cost	**Budget £**	**Actual £**	**Variance £**	**Adverse/ Favourable**
Water	600	625	25	Adverse
Marshals	720	630	90	Favourable

Workings

Budgeted water cost: 1,200 runners × £0.50 = £600

Budgeted marshals cost: (1,200 / 100) × £60 = £720

2

Output	Fixed costs £	Variable costs £	Total costs £	Unit cost £
3,000 units	36,000	9,000	45,000	15.00
8,000 units	36,000	24,000	60,000	7.50
10,000 units	36,000	30,000	66,000	6.60

Workings

Variable costs:

3,000 × £3 = £9,000

8,000 × £3 = £24,000

10,000 × £3 = £30,000

From:	A Student
To:	Finance Director
Sent:	1 December 20X8
Subject:	Variances

Many organisations have what is known as a 'standard cost' for items they produce, setting out what they expect each unit to cost in terms of materials and labour and fixed overhead. This standard cost is then multiplied by the number of items expected to be produced in order to estimate expected figures.

Comparison of expected figures with actual results is an extremely important tool for management in their control of the business. The differences between the actual costs and income and the budgeted costs and income are known as variances. These can be adverse ('bad' for the business) or favourable ('good' for the business).

Any significant variances should be reported to management as a priority, as the reasons for them must be investigated and corrective action taken.

Normally the managers of a business only wish to be informed about significant variances, by means of a variance report or significance report.

The significance of a variance cannot be determined simply by its size – the size of the variance must be compared with the budgeted amount. For example, a variance of £10,000 is tiny if the budgeted amount is £1,000,000 but is huge if the budgeted amount is only £15,000.

Therefore the significance of a variance will often be determined by measuring it as a percentage of the budgeted figure. If it is more than, say, 10% of the budgeted amount then the organisation's policy may be that it must be reported to management.

Glossary of terms

It is useful to be familiar with interchangeable terminology including IFRS and UK GAAP (generally accepted accounting principles).

Below is a short list of the most important terms you are likely to use or come across, together with their international and UK equivalents.

UK term	International term
Profit and loss account	**Statement of profit or loss (or statement of profit or loss and other comprehensive income)**
Turnover or Sales	Revenue or Sales Revenue
Operating profit	Profit from operations
Reducing balance depreciation	Diminishing balance depreciation
Depreciation / depreciation expense(s)	Depreciation charge(s)
Balance sheet	**Statement of financial position**
Fixed assets	Non-current assets
Net book value	Carrying amount
Tangible assets	Property, plant and equipment
Stocks	Inventories
Trade debtors or Debtors	Trade receivables
Prepayments	Other receivables
Debtors and prepayments	Trade and other receivables
Cash at bank and in hand	Cash and cash equivalents
Long-term liabilities	Non-current liabilities
Trade creditors or creditors	Trade payables
Accruals	Other payables
Creditors and accruals	Trade and other payables
Capital and reserves	Equity (limited companies)
Profit and loss balance	Retained earnings
Cash flow statement	**Statement of cash flows**

Accountants often have a tendency to use several phrases to describe the same thing! Some of these are listed below:

Different terms for the same thing
Nominal ledger, main ledger or general ledger
Subsidiary ledgers, memorandum ledgers
Subsidiary (sales) ledger, sales ledger
Subsidiary (purchases) ledger, purchases ledger

Index

L

Labour, 103
Liabilities, 7, 12
LIFO (last in, first out), 78, 94
Limited company, 3, 12
Limited liability, 3

M

Management accounting, 8, 12
Management accounts, 8
Manufacturing account, 87, 94
Manufacturing cost, 94
Manufacturing organisation, 12
Materials, 69
Materials requisition, 70, 71, 94

N

National Insurance, 105
Non-current assets, 17
Numeric coding, 31, 43

O

OAR, 112
Overhead absorption rate, 110, 112, 116
Overheads, 22, 26, 103, 111
Overtime, 103
Overtime premium, 103, 104, 116
Overtime time rate, 116

P

Partnership, 3, 12
Payable, 12
Payables, 5
Period costs, 54, 63
Piecework, 106, 116
Planning, 8
Prime cost, 22, 26
Production cost centres, 24
Profit centre, 24, 26
Profit maximisation, 24
Purchase order, 71
Purchase requisition, 70, 71
Purpose of accounting, 6

R

Raw materials, 69
Receivable, 12
Receivables, 5
Remuneration methods, 103
Responsibility centre, 26
Responsibility centres, 23
Retail, 4
Retail organisation, 12
Revenue expenditure, 5, 17, 26
Revenue transactions, 12

S

Salary, 109
Semi-variable cost, 51
Semi-variable costs, 55, 63
Service cost centres, 24
Service organisation, 12
Significance of a variance, 126
Significance report, 126, 130
Sole trader, 3, 12
Standard cost, 121, 130
Statement of financial position, 7, 12
Statement of profit or loss, 7, 12
Stores ledger account, 70

T

Time rate, 103, 116
Trade payable, 5
Trade receivable, 5
Types of business transactions, 4

U

Unit cost, 63
Unit product cost, 90, 94

V

Variable cost, 51
Variable costs, 63
Variance report, 126, 130
Variances, 121, 130

W

Work in progress (WIP), 69

Notes

REVIEW FORM

How have you used this Course Book?
(Tick one box only)

☐ Self study

☐ On a course_____

☐ Other _____

Why did you decide to purchase this Course Book? *(Tick one box only)*

☐ Have used BPP materials in the past

☐ Recommendation by friend/colleague

☐ Recommendation by a college lecturer

☐ Saw advertising

☐ Other _____

During the past six months do you recall seeing/receiving either of the following?
(Tick as many boxes as are relevant)

☐ Our advertisement in Accounting Technician

☐ Our Publishing Catalogue

Which (if any) aspects of our advertising do you think are useful?
(Tick as many boxes as are relevant)

☐ Prices and publication dates of new editions

☐ Information on Course Book content

☐ Details of our free online offering

☐ None of the above

Your ratings, comments and suggestions would be appreciated on the following areas of this Course Book.

	Very useful	Useful	Not useful
Chapter overviews	☐	☐	☐
Introductory section	☐	☐	☐
Quality of explanations	☐	☐	☐
Illustrations	☐	☐	☐
Chapter activities	☐	☐	☐
Test your learning	☐	☐	☐
Keywords	☐	☐	☐

	Excellent	Good	Adequate	Poor
Overall opinion of this Course Book	☐	☐	☐	☐

Do you intend to continue using BPP Products?   ☐ Yes ☐ No

Please note any further comments and suggestions/errors on the reverse of this page. The BPP author of this edition can be emailed at: lmfeedback@bpp.com.

Alternatively, the Head of Programme of this edition can be emailed at: nisarahmed@bpp.com

REVIEW FORM (continued)

TELL US WHAT YOU THINK

Please note any further comments and suggestions/errors below